COVENANT
OF THE GENERATIONS

Publication of *Covenant of the Generations* was made possible
through the generous contributions of:

**CONGREGATION SCHAARAI ZEDEK SISTERHOOD
TAMPA, FLORIDA**

———— ❧ ————

LYNN MAGID LAZAR AND DALE S. LAZAR

———— ❧ ————

**NORMA U. LEVITT PUBLICATION FUND OF
WOMEN OF REFORM JUDAISM**

COVENANT
OF THE GENERATIONS

New Prayers, Poems,
and Meditations
from
Women of
Reform Judaism

Women of Reform Judaism

Printed in the United States of America

18 17 16 15 14 13   1 2 3 4 5 6

This paper meets the requirements of ANSI/NISO.
The stocks used in the printing of this book are FSC certified.

ISBN-13: 978-0-9884639-0-5
Library of Congress Control Number: 2012954146

Published by:
Women of Reform Judaism
633 Third Avenue
New York, NY 10017-6778
Phone: 212.650.4050   Fax: 212.650.4059
E-mail: info@wrj.org
Website: www.wrj.org

In celebration of the Centennial
of Women of Reform Judaism,
this book is dedicated to:

The generations of women past,
who laid the sturdy foundation for
Women of Reform Judaism
and the National Federation
of Temple Sisterhoods,
upon whose shoulders we stand;

The generations of women present,
who work daily to enrich WRJ,
our sisterhoods and congregations,
the institutions of Reform Judaism,
and the world at large,
allowing us to thrive as we
fulfill the historic mission of
Women of Reform Judaism; and

The generations of women to come,
who will chart a new course
for our next hundred years,
while remaining ever true to
our fundamental values.

WOMEN OF
REFORM JUDAISM

YEARS STRONG

Inspired by the past.
Committed to the future.

Other books in the Covenant Book Series
by Women of Reform Judaism:

Covenant of the Heart

Covenant of the Soul

Covenant of the Spirit

CONTENTS

FOREWORD

In the hearts, souls, and spirits of those whose wisdom and loving strength are an eternal blessing: A Covenant of the Generations.

~ Rabbi Rachel Hertzman

This newest volume in our Covenant Book series has been published in celebration of the centennial of Women of Reform Judaism. Since 1913, women's groups and sisterhoods of Reform congregations have joined together to support and enrich the Reform Movement, first as the National Federation of Temple Sisterhoods (NFTS) and more recently as Women of Reform Judaism (WRJ). Stronger together, Reform Jewish women have helped build the institutional structures of Reform Judaism, funded clergy training, educated our religious school children, and supported our teens as they grow to become the next generation of leaders.

Among WRJ's most prominent accomplishments has been elevating the voice of women in religious and spiritual realms. When NFTS was first established, women could not serve on congregational boards or in Reform Movement leadership. They had no recognized role in crafting the language of prayer, creating Movement liturgy, or leading worship. In many instances, they were not even permitted on the bimah. Over the course of the past hundred years, NFTS and WRJ worked vigorously to advocate for the changes that would bring women fully into the religious life of our Reform Jewish community, tackling one major hurdle at a time, seeking transformation from within.

In 1948, NFTS published its first book of prayers to provide "fitting language" and "rich poetry of devotion" for women's spiritual expression. In 1993, when we changed our name to Women of Reform Judaism, we published the first book in our Covenant Series, *Covenant of the Heart*, followed by *Covenant of the Soul* (2000) and *Covenant of the Spirit* (2005). Both then and now, these inspiring collections reflect the timeless need of women to share their spiritual yearnings and personal prayers in their own voices. Written by women, for women, the pieces speak to the joys, struggles, special moments, and sacred journeys of women throughout the generations.

We hope you will be uplifted and moved by the poetic and passionate voices of the women who have shared their personal reflections within these pages. We are grateful for the beautiful treasure they have bequeathed to us. This gift is now yours to use and enjoy.

Covenant of the Generations is dedicated to the generations of women past, present, and future, who have brought us to this moment in our history, and who will lead us into the future. Women are, and always will be, stronger together.

Lynn Magid Lazar
President
Women of Reform Judaism

Rabbi Marla J. Feldman
Executive Director
Women of Reform Judaism

January 2013

SISTERHOOD: A COVENANT OF THE GENERATIONS

We gave up our hand mirrors to the covenant builders so long ago. Each moment that we nurture the promise anew we search for our reflections

In the glistening eyes of our mothers, daughters, partners, sisters. Overflowing with gratitude and grief, pain and triumph

In wax-encrusted fingernails held up to flickering light

In notes scrawled on discarded to-do lists, faded recipes, dream journal pages left open on bedside tables

In wellsprings of memory
Stolen glances behind looking glass covers
Seeking what we have lost and who we are becoming

In still, small moments of peace
In whirling celebration

In the hearts, souls, and spirits of those whose wisdom and loving strength are an eternal blessing: A Covenant of the Generations

~ *Rabbi Rachel Hertzman*

LIVING

OUR COVENANT

SISTERHOOD

WOMEN OF REFORM JUDAISM

SISTERHOOD

The Twenty-First Century Jewish Woman

Her personal shadow holds hands
With her collective shadow
And sisters unite.

She is a lawyer, a doctor, a banker, a teacher,
A nurse, a mother, a rabbi, a volunteer.

The Jewish woman bakes challah,
Cooks chicken soup, knits for patients,
Serves her temple, stands for right.

She prays for peace, raises her children,
Creates beauty, entertains her guests.

Devoted to Jewish thought
She teaches Torah, feeds the homeless,
Sends greetings to those who live alone.

The Jewish woman lives to mend
Our ailing world. And the Shechinah smiles.

My Sisters

Challenge me when I am too safe
    Enlighten me when I am confused
        Encourage me when I fear to fail
            Champion me when I stumble
                Support me when I grieve
                    Bless me with your love

Being Part of a Sacred Community

Being part of this special, sacred group of women ...

Allows me to share ideas that sustain and promote
the ideals of sisterhood
       in the midst of women in my community.

I feel proud ... I am blessed ... I am a better woman
       because of these women who are my friends.
I have an opportunity to encourage others to be
the best they can be
       as our greater group builds connections.

I feel the strength and bonds of women
       that link me to the generations before and yet to be.
I feel at one with our matriarchs.
Sisterhood gives me a sense of continuity to all the sisters
who have led
       me to this place in this time.

I am fortunate to call these women sisters.
I am in awe of their commitment.
I am grateful for this sense of family, Jewish family.

This special, sacred group of women teaches me about myself;
       they inspire me to be the best I can be.
Together, we build mitzvah and memory and the future.

This Is Sisterhood

We are each of us unique, but we do not stand alone.
When joy abounds for one of us, we all celebrate;
When sorrow envelops one of us, we all shed tears.

> This is Sisterhood.

We are each of us unique, but we do not stand alone.
When success comes to one of us, we all rejoice;
When failure reaches one of us, we all strive to recover.

> This is Sisterhood.

We are each of us unique, but we do not stand alone.
When one of us gives birth, we all share the simcha;
When death descends in our midst, we are all diminished.

> This is Sisterhood.

We are each of us unique, but we do not stand alone.
When one of us chooses to pursue a goal,
    we band together in common purpose.
When one of us finds the path too steep,
    we push and pull together in common strength.

> This is Sisterhood.

We bring to each other the warmth of family.
We share in the presence and the promise of each other.
We gather strength from the past to develop faith in the future.

> This is Sisterhood.

Of Sisters

Of sisters, I am one of three
One older, one younger
The bonds are from birth and will never be severed.

Of sisters, I am one of many
Some older, some younger
We work together for our sisterhood, community and temple.

Of sisters, I am one of a multitude
Some older, some younger
We strive to ensure the future of our faith and our movement.

My birth sisters were given to me
I sought out the others
In kitchens, in meetings, in workshops and programs.
They join me in song, they join me in dance—
They join me in tears and they join me in laughter
They offer me friendship, and support dreams of the future.

My life has been blessed by all of my sisters
By birth and by choice
My world is enhanced and my spirit uplifted
By the women who I am privileged to refer to as "sister."

Sisters by Choice

We are sisters by choice. We have chosen to be there for each other, and at the end of our days the friendships that we have made will be as important as the relationships that we are born into.

Sisterhood gives us an amazing amount of strength to face the things that come before us that are seemingly not faceable at the time.

Often I think of my ancestors who are linking me to the past, but it is my sisters who are linking me to the future. We get to our future together by joining our hands together in sisterhood.

The Light of God

I sit at the table
With my Sisters
And I see
The Light of God
In their eyes.

Each one comes
With their special gifts
Their valued opinions
Beliefs and intentions
To build and improve
A sacred community
Embracing the work
The vision
With laughter and grace.

And it will be
Very Good
Because I see
The Light of God
In their eyes.

Fertile Ground

Fertile ground
A packet of seeds
A shovel and a hoe
A full watering can
Sunshine and rain
Warm weather
Loving care
Seedlings
Sprouts
Plants
Fruit of love
Sisters
Meetings
Committees
New friendships
The strong bonds
The helping hands
Love and support
Praying together
Blooming lives
Enriching us

Sarah's Tent

We stand together
in the light of a Sunday morning
Our bodies are exhausted
yet our minds exhilarated

From a weekend of sharing and praying
laughing and crying
singing, our voices radiant and one
Us girls

We arrived in the rain
spilling stories of anguish
Troubled children and ailing parents
painful losses, breast cancer
Helping each other through

We chanted Torah
and discussed its meaning
We danced
We played silly games until the wee hours
and devoured sweets without remorse

The waves of the winter ocean
calmed our souls
Blue heaven
as we huddled close
shivering under our jackets and scarves
on a Shabbat that will live on in our hearts

Now
before we go home
we toss a ball of yarn from one to another
back and forth
describing our friendships
old and new

The thread winds its way around the room
the ball becoming smaller
as each shares what she has experienced
on our journey

It takes time
our backs begin to ache
Yet we don't want to finish
We hold onto the energy

In the end
we raise the web of emotions high into the air
We look up, and we see it
what we have created

Sarah's Tent encircles us all
it covers our heads
Shimmering in the sunshine, it welcomes us, protects us
and strengthens us

There is a safety, an intimacy among women
it is hard to describe, but easy to feel
It is sacred, holy
Today and tomorrow
it is Sisterhood

Our Divine Spark

Each of us has a Divine Spark within.
Our very own piece of the shattered vessel,
Striving to be reunited to create a better world.
Like the Ner Tamid, it is ever present inside
When we are rejoicing,
When we are in mourning,
When we are laughing,
When we are praying,
When we are in need,
And when we are fulfilled.
Sometimes a quiet hum, yet often a loud noise,
Always propelling us forward, never separated from our being.
We are the keepers of our light in search of a perfect world.

As Sisters, we come together
Creating a brighter fire in each of us,
Burning our unique flames
Like a twisted Havdalah candle
That secures its life from each individual wick,
Putting together the pieces that make us complete
When we are baking,
When we are planning,
When we are dancing,
When we are crying,
When we are helping others,
And when we link arms in Sisterhood.
Our Eternal Flames shine brighter,
Our purpose is stamped out through community,
And our lives are enriched by Tikkun Olam,
Bringing the Divine that much closer to us all.

WOMEN OF REFORM JUDAISM

A Sanctuary for Our Jewish Lives

Sisterhood provides a Sanctuary for our Jewish lives.
Within the arms of Sisterhood we find:
The sacredness of friendship;
The refuge of our history;
The consecration of mission;
And, the altar of leadership.

We are strengthened by the obligations of our faith:
To honor father and mother
To perform acts of love and kindness
To attend the house of study daily
To welcome the stranger
To visit the sick
To rejoice with the bride and groom
To console the bereaved
To pray with sincerity

We are rich in history,
righteous in principles,
rewarded in the quality of life
We are Women of Reform Judaism—Women of Sisterhood.

We are Grandmothers, Mothers, Sisters, Aunts, Daughters,
Wives, Friends, Women of the Covenant.
We are Deborah, Rachel, Leah, Rebecca, Sarah,
Hannah, Ruth, and Miriam.
We are Women of Sisterhood—Women of Reform Judaism.

To the tent of meeting we bring an ancient faith,
For the sake of that faith we come to the tent of meeting.
For the sake of that faith we welcome the stranger.
For the sake of that faith we remember:
Sinai, Auschwitz, and Jerusalem.
For the sake of that faith we say: "*Am Yisrael Chai.*"

Woman to woman, each pair of hands lifts another.
Woman to woman, each heart beats the melody of life.
Woman to woman, each voice joins another in song.
Woman to woman, each teaches another, each guides another.
Woman to woman, each of us gives voice to dreams.
Woman to woman, each of us recognizes the links between
past and future.
We know who we are and what we can become.
Woman to woman we seek the qualities of
strength and sensitivity,
courage and charm,
performance and potential,
nurturing and need,
vision and value.

We make Sisterhood a Sanctuary for our Jewish lives.

The Feeling of Sisterhood

Like Miriam and her sisters dancing
with singular intent
Or Dinah and her friends sharing stories
in the red tent
Like our foresisters before us as they
crossed the Red Sea
That's the feeling of Sisterhood, the power of unity.

Like Bella Abzug and her comrades
In their unique, New York fashion
Serving the common good
United in passion
Or Golda Meir whose vision
Propelled an entire society
That's the feeling of Sisterhood,
The magic of solidarity.

Then there's the sisters you know, who you meet everyday
Not larger than life, but giving, each in her way
Serving with purpose, enhancing the community
That's the feeling of Sisterhood, the blessing of camaraderie.

Sisterhood—
It's the feeling you get
When you know you belong
And the rush of fulfillment
When we're 65,000 strong
And the satisfaction of being a part of a greater social good
That's the joy of WRJ, the chemistry of Sisterhood.

Pursuing Justice

There is no better way to make Torah come alive
Than in following the path of *Pursuing Justice*

Pioneer women of the Reform Movement ... even before 1913,
     led the way
NFTS in the day and now WRJ

The rights of women from voting to equality to choice ...
     to having a voice
The safety and protection of the children ... the most important
     hope of our future
The embrace of the Jewish soldiers ... the men and women who
     protect our freedoms
The support of Israel ... and especially its girls and women

From founding the Jewish Braille Institute with actions to help
     the visually impaired
To advocating against barriers for all who are
     physically challenged
From being first in line to promote stem cell research and
     therapeutic cloning
To advocating for the rights of the lesbian and gay community
And on and on and on as women who lead the way in *tikkun olam,*
     repairing the world

Pursuing Justice is a way of life
WRJ models it for women ... for the world
Helping all people live stronger together
And always being aware and keeping the circle open for inclusion

There is no better way to make Torah come alive
Than in following the path of *Pursuing Justice*

A Tree of Life

In God's glory a sapling grows.

The thin trunk is blessed to stand upright.

As its trunk expands, it begins to branch out in splendor, growing higher and higher, near and far.

Yet its prevailing trunk has to weather storms and obstacles as it struggles for continual progress.

More and more branches appear outward, upward, toward the heavens as if to thank God for all its strength and direction.

Its branches sway gently in the wind creating an amalgam of sound while life pulses through its body and soul—its spirit entwined through the labyrinth of its intricate root system.

As the sun shines through from above, a minuscule amount of foliage appears.

As the years pass, the foliage grows heroically.

And still, additional branches develop leaving room for more foliage.

The growth is of magnificent beauty, varying contours and dimensions growing out from one powerful source.

As 100 years arise, the leaves multiply even more brilliantly, but still allowing space for increasing development.

Determined, it soars, rooting itself firmly.

But even as it grows with fervor, the need for nurturing remains essential.

It rids itself of the faltering branches in order for the rest to remain sturdy.

Its entire essence increases, constantly challenging its path, as it continues to grow in majesty and humility.

This is God's blessing and our gift from generations past.

And so, we must repeatedly maintain its evolution in the spirit of joy and enthusiasm.

We are the cultivators. We are the custodians.

WE ARE THE WOMEN OF REFORM JUDAISM.

On Becoming a Leader

Becoming a leader is a sacred honor
Following in the footsteps of those who came before us
Accepting the legacies that made it possible for us to be here
Paving the way for those who follow to do more
Continuing the task that we can only begin to complete
Honoring God, ourselves and each other.

L'dor vador we accept this torch
We will lift it proudly and carry it high
From Sarah, Rebeccah, Rachel and Leah

(*continued*)

To their daughters, through the generations
To our grandmothers, our mothers and on to us
The lifeblood of Judaism is now in our hands
The strength of us all will keep it lit.

We stand here together before God,
Making an oath to be our best
To do what is right,
To forge a new path,
To lead by example
And show others the way.

We stand with each other,
Facing our challenges,
Working together,
Sharing ideas,
Building bridges,
Helping ourselves,
For the greater good.

May we be blessed as we accept this task
May we have strength when we stumble
May we have courage to create a better tomorrow
And may we all remember that while the world was created
For us alone, we are but ashes and dust, stronger together.

CELEBRATING

OUR COVENANT

SHABBAT

HOLIDAYS

SHABBAT

Preparing for Shabbat

I have time today to shop in an unhurried way for
Shabbat dinner.
After I check out, I realize that it would be nice to have flowers;
I have time to go back to buy flowers.
This doesn't happen every Friday.
I delight in these times when I can focus on Shabbat.

I have time today to cook Shabbat dinner in a calm way.
Even having time to remember what I sometimes forget.
Would that I could mark each Shabbat with intention
But I will not dwell now on other Shabbats;
I will delight in preparing for this one.

Become One

Shabbat returns, the week comes to an end
      go ahead
           take a breath
              take a few
                 slow down
             allow Shabbat to wash over you
         become one with the stillness
     and welcome that extra soul into your life

Turning Point

Sky turning from blue to ruby to sapphire,
At last the moment has arrived,
This is the turning point,
Outside, the day turns to night and
within, within, our souls turn to
embrace the sweetness that is Shabbat.

I light the Shabbat candles
and ignite the fire of my soul.
I say the b'rachah
and hear the voice within respond.
I feel my soul gates open
to let the Sabbath in.

And the darkness of evening
becomes the light of Shabbat,
And from the inner stillness,
my soul begins to dance.

Shabbat Prayer

Sacred space — Lighting the candles opens the doorway to
my sacred space. I close my eyes, feel the warmth of the flame,
hear the sacred words coming from within and blend with the
voices of my family. Together we chant as mothers and families
have chanted for generations, the same chant, the same
sacred words. As the quiet re-emerges, with eyes still closed,
I visualize my children, my husband, my parents now long gone
and offer them the peace of Shabbat.

Gather in Shabbat

Gather all ye assembled. Gather in close.
As we stand here side by side, shoulder to shoulder
Our thoughts turn from the world outside to that faith and
hope we hold dear.
Feel the presence of the sweet Shabbat upon us.
Open our hearts and let it in.
Embrace the warmth and joy it brings to us all.
Sing out from our hearts the prayers of old.
Let us feel the air dance with the presence of Shabbat.
Feel the joy of sisters, community, family, and Torah.
Let it spill over into all our days and fill our hearts
with gladness.
Gather to you all the wonders and sweetness of this Shabbat.
And hold its sweetness close.

Shabbat

How lovely the pure translucent water
Pouring over my hands, the quiet entering my soul's depth
Tranquil feeling of safety
Candlelight illuminating
All darkness dispelled for a time
Friends and Family who touch my inner self.
Thank you, God, for creating this time
To restore, to prepare, to strengthen
For that unknown which is to come.

Zachor

Newspapers covering the kitchen floor
The distinctive aroma as I walk through the door.
        Zachor–Remember.

If I close my eyes I can continue the tour
Off to the side the shadows of the past
spill into the now empty places
        And I remember.

The spoon resting in the luchen–
waiting to be served with the chicken soup–
or perhaps,
Waiting for me to sneak a not so unexpected taste.

The beautiful handwoven tablecloth,
The brass candlesticks signaling the glow of the approaching day.
I watch this silent movie play through my mind and
I can be there again.

The embracing of the Sabbath lights
The same warm embrace encircling me
in my grandmother's arms.
She who taught me of the Cossacks, a bissel Yiddish,
The prayer for rising in the morning and the one for a rainbow,
About tzedakah as she placed the coins in the pishke,
About our history, our traditions . . .
The empty well in my heart fills with memories.

Zachor–remember.
Shamor–keep–I keep the Sabbath and guard its memories and
Pray that my children will one day remember
As they too light the same brass candlesticks
Which my grandmother and her grandmother before her
stood and kindled.

Shabbos

Candles
 We form for you
 a small sukkah
 with our hands
 a shelter while you
 are small
 Till you are strong
 Then leave you to
 illumine all you may
 Take your gift of
 light and heat
 into ourselves
 Till we too
 grow strong

Wine
 Uplifted fruit of the earth
 candlelight glows through you
 Our song lifts higher
 with each phrase
 praise for the goodness
 of the world and
 of the spirit,
 the beauty of this day

Challah
 Fragrant hopeful
 twists and turns
 We come together
 to pull you apart
 Nourish ourselves
 and each other

Turn from outward to in
from tense to soft
from work to each other
worry to warmth
perhaps even
to laughter

For Shabbat

Holy One of Being,
Help us replace
The earthbound things,
Confines of space,
With Sabbath eyes,
With Sabbath heart.

Help us to climb,
To reach that place
In sacred time
Where we can find
Our Sabbath soul.

Help us, we pray,
To recognize
Your Holiness,
To sanctify
And to embrace
The Sabbath day,
Your precious gift,
With love and grace.

Kol Isha Prayer for Candle Lighting

We light these candles
to honour our voices,
Kol Isha, women's voices
in prayer and song.
> *We light these candles*
> *for the women of the Torah,*
> *for the women of our history,*
> *for the women who touch our lives.*

We light these candles
for the women of honour,
living and dead.
They are with us tonight,
enfolded in the sanctuaries of our hearts,
their presence no farther away
than a heartbeat, a soulbeat.
> *We light these candles*
> *as a symbol*
> *of our faith,*
> *our hopes, our dreams,*
> *our possibilities.*

HOLIDAYS

Washing Windows in Elul

Prepping
for Rosh Hashanah
begins in Elul
the month
of pulling cobwebs
from vows
we promised to fulfill
in the fading year.

Washing windows
in Elul
redirects reflection
of my inward eye
to the hands-in-water task
of wiping clear
the splotches
marring
an outward view.

I gather my supplies—
water bucket spiked
with splash of vinegar,
dishtowels saved for scrubbing,
newsprint for streakless shine,
ladder to allow
a rise to heights above
my normal reach.

Accumulations since
the rituals of spring—
grime from dusty wind,
splatterings from rain
propel me into motion.

I rub until
through sparkling glass
I see outside the window
the blessings
in my garden
rising
like a silent prayer—
the slow release of summer
robed in flames of fall.

Swishing water in my bucket,
squeezing out my rag,
stirs me
like the season,
to embrace a turn,

in the sounding
of the shofar
to heed the crying
in our world of tears,

and hear anew
Isaiah's message
bleating through
the ancient horn—

> Dig deep in neglected gardens
> Sow seeds of repair
> Plant and tend and harvest
> *G'mar chatimah tovah*
> a year inscribed for good.

The Sound of Shofar

Hear now the rousing sound of shofar
reminding us of God's presence
when we were young at Sinai,
how the blaring of the ram's horn
filled our hearts with breathless wonder
as God offered us the Torah
and bound us together in love.

Hear now the bleating sound of shofar
recalling God's recurring mercy
how at the altar on Moriah
a ram ended Abraham's anguish,
ended Isaac's binding pain.
Hear now the blaring call to freedom,
hear the yearning sound of hope.

Hear now the weeping sound of shofar
joining us to other generations:
to the prayers of all our fathers
to the sound of a mother's tears.
Let it wake us now from slumber
as we turn again toward God.

For God hears the urgent sound of shofar.
It is the sound of all our voices
primordial and pleading
through all the generations
piercing the very soul of time
to reach the heart of God.

Here I Am, God

Here I am, God,
Here I am again
In this warm and holy place
Where songs of the seasons flow.
Here I am again
Stumbling and struggling
On the journey that never ends
But begins at this moment:
This moment as I turn to You
Humbly and filled with awe,
Asking forgiveness
With fresh acts of atonement.
God, Your love gives me hope once more
That I can begin again.
For this day marks the dawn of time;
It is the moment of my birth again,
The new year of my soul.
Here I am, God.
Hineni.

Kol Nidrei

Look, I scream "Outrage!" and I am not answered,
I shout and there is no justice....
[God] uprooted my hope like a tree.

(Job 19: 7, 10)

I am feeling last minute about everything this year.
And so, in the shower, before I go to bed, I decide that, for
me, Yom Kippur will start in the morning.
Because, well, I'm in the shower, for starters.
Because I spent the evening playing with my eleven-month-old
son and putting him to bed.
Because I ate crackers and drank mint tea
after the sun went down.
Because I watched *Kol Nidrei* services streaming on a webcast
while putting the finishing touches on Yom Kippur morning
family *t'filah*.

It seems to me that God is feeling last minute about her
Yom Kippur preparations too since the tornado that swept
through my neighborhood happened poetically,
almost crudely,
the day before Yom Kippur.

The news keeps repeating "only one fatality."
One last person will not be sealed in the Book of Life.
I guess I understand, given the severity of the damage, "only"
one death seems disproportionate to the wrath of the storm.
I didn't know the woman who died. Was it even a woman?
I'm not sure.
But I do know she was driving home from work when a tree
came through her car window.
A tree from a tornado in Brooklyn.

And I imagine that the people who loved her aren't relieved
that there was "only" one fatality.
My guess is that they are not so thrilled
with God's last minute antics.
Not at all.

My husband said he couldn't get into the Yom Kippur spirit
this year.
And I almost agreed with him.
But then, right outside the window in the baby's room
this evening,
as everyone else's—but not my—Yom Kippur was starting,
I noticed a wood-chipper truck.
The workmen feeding broken branches,
leaves,
stumps,
and twigs
to the grinding, unforgiving teeth of the machine.
Less than 24 hours had passed since the tornado tore
the trees down—
their leaves still healthy and green—
and already they were being turned into mulch.
How Jewish.
I felt sad for the trees.
Mournful actually.
Angry at God.

What's the point of that commuter's death?
Why kill so many trees?
The spirit of Yom Kippur slowly descends on me.
Who by fire, who by water . . .

Yom Kippur

Saturday
Kids on the streets
Riding their bikes
Not a car
In sight
Fasting
On this
Holiest of days
Me
One of many
All
Fasting
Reflecting
The country
Shut down
For a day
One day
When all are equal
Before the eyes
Of G-d
Walking
In Jerusalem
In the middle
Of a highway
Down to

The forest
Stopping
At a playground
Sliding
Feeling young
Then old
Hiking down
Seeing
Where the war
Was fought
And the rocks
Painted
White and blue
Seeing
The garbage
Carelessly dropped
Walking home
Slowly
Past
Children
On their bikes
Adults watching
Sometimes joining in
Past
The crowded shuls

Full to bursting
The chanting
Audible
Across the street
Past
The single car
Driving down the
Street
Feeling that flash
Of disgust
Who is he?
This man
To drive today?
To be so arrogant?
But
It's Yom Kippur
So I forgive
Go home
Thinking
About this strange day
Once a year
Me
And us all

Sonnet on the Book of Life

They say the book's been open these ten days
and that's when God inscribes us for good or ill.
I say the book of life is open always
and in it I write according to my will—
composing or reworking, in control
of every nicely done or faulty line.
I'm never satisfied, but on the whole
I'm sure each chapter, good or bad, is mine:
until some interruption comes. A mind?
a senseless accident? will jog my pen
and force upon my work a cruel or kind
new twist—a loss, a gift, a shocking end.
When careful plan and fate fall out of sync,
don't drop the pen, write on, but change the ink.

Pesach *Yizkor*

The dining room table was simply resplendent. Covered in her now off-white lace table cloth, the oak wooden table stood sturdily atop the navy tuft pile carpet, though every year a few more shims were added for leveling. On the soft carpet, slight impressions from hundreds of chair legs left indented memories of the past.

In the corners of the dining room, white built-in cabinets displayed china dishes with tiny blue and white flowers, wine glasses of every size, a shelf reserved entirely for Shabbat candlesticks, and a rudimentary Chanukkah menorah made of wood and bolts, the sole survivor of Sunday school, now coated with wax.

The door was open to Elijah. At one end of the table, sat his goblet full of wine, waiting for his visit, while across from it, Miriam's cup stood in prominence. The children, who were now adults, still shot furtive glances at these cups. Would the wine disappear this year like it always had?

As in every year, there was too much food. He always cooked for twelve, even though now, there were only five or six people who might return to this table for Passover.

In the foyer, a few table leaves leaned against a corner.
   "Honey, we don't need them this year," he suggested to his wife.
   "No. Let's put them in—just in case."
   "But Mom," their adult children echoed, "it's just the six of us. And the leaves are really heavy. It's not worth breaking your back over."
   "No. No. Let's put them in—just in case."
And so they compromised. This year, one leaf would be used. The other would stand lonely in another room.
   "And Mom, we don't need extra chairs either."

It's in these moments, joyous holiday meals and family celebrations, that we remember them. It is in the smell of spices so fragrant, the taste of sweet wine and the shadow of candles flickering, that we recall the days when they sat next to us and sometimes we can still feel their warmth.

As we recall the story of the Jewish people, of our redemption from slavery in Egypt, we remember also the story of our own families: the journeys and experiences that shaped us, the people and places, and the faces that sat across from us, shared meals with us, shared the story with us—for so many years.

We can't help but want to set a place for them at the table, hoping that they will walk in the door years after they've departed. We can't help but want to hear their voices singing, laughing. We can't help want to smell their perfume, to taste their cooking, to see their smile.

While our memories are but meager substitute for the warm hug we so long to experience, may we find solace and comfort in knowing that while they may be gone, our memories endure.

Strangers on the Seder Plate

I do not remember one,
but surely there was a seder plate
with the essential symbols—
shank bone, roasted egg,
charoset, bitter herb and greens—

on my grandmother's table
where the family gathered
to celebrate the night
different from all others,

probably just one
of the Passover dishes
she hauled out before the holiday
and after the week of eating *pesadich*
packed away again

and not a plate like mine,
crafted in pottery,
each symbol molded
in its own compartment
beneath its Hebrew name,
elevating its importance
to the ritual telling
of the exodus from slavery
to desert wandering.

What would she think
of the additions—
plagues her granddaughter
two generations later
has included
on her own seder plate:

olives for those that could not ripen
on ancient trees uprooted
for a divisive wall

cocoa beans for children
forced to labor
splitting hulls
with a machete
and prying out the seeds

an orange with audacious color
among the monotones
for a call to women
excluded in the past
to document their presence
in a new Haggadah text.

Would she understand
the strange inclusions?
Could she imagine they are there
to fulfill the obligation
to go forth into the broken world
still needing our repair?

The Four WRJ Daughters

This is my tale of four WRJ daughters: The wise one, the wicked one, the simple one, and the young one.

The wise daughter wants to know about WRJ and what it does, because she wants to be a member. Unto her I say, "WRJ started in 1913 when 156 women from fifty-two Reform congregations met to form an organization to meet the needs of Reform women's groups in North America. Since then, the organization has grown to 65,000 women representing 500 groups all over the world. Together, we work to ensure the future of Reform Judaism."

The wicked daughter thinks WRJ has no relevance to her. Unto her I say, "The rabbi and cantor you rely on received an excellent education because of WRJ support. The social justice issues you should care about are given a loud and clear voice because of WRJ involvement. The Reform Jewish summer camp you loved benefited from funds WRJ provided for camp projects and scholarships. I could go on and tell you how much the WRJ women of your temple do for your congregation, but suffice it to say that WRJ has been a relevant factor in your life as a Reform Jew whether you know it or not."

The simple daughter does not know how to ask about WRJ. Unto her I say, "Please come and join us. We want you to be part of this important group that supports our congregation and Reform Judaism everywhere. We want you to enjoy friendships not only within our local group, but also those you can make on a district and worldwide level. We want you to experience the pride of being part of an organization that keeps Reform Judaism thriving. I will be happy to pick you up, and we can go together!"

The last daughter is the young one. Unto her I say,
"The future of WRJ is in your hands. We give you a solid
foundation, the result of one hundred years of commitment
to training future WRJ and congregation leaders, to
educating future clergy, to advocating for social justice,
to supporting our youth, and to raising funds to run our
programs. We hope you will continue this work and build
upon it as you guide WRJ through the twenty-first century.
Our motto is, 'Stronger Together.' We hope you will
remember it as you make our organization yours.
It will serve you well."

Now my tale is told.

The Journey Never Ends

The journey never ends.

We are forever leaving Egypt
    and returning.
Our souls are still groping
for meaning in desert dust.
Echoes of that first Seder
in the wilderness of our freedom
continue to haunt us.
Where was our home?
The taste of hot sand chafed our lips
nostalgic for the smells of Egypt.
How could we know
that our discomfort was our freedom?

We are forever leaving Egypt.
Like spring's first seedlings
rescued from winter's wrath,
nurtured by April rain,
we emerge from our bondage
redeemed from our discontent
and the slavery of dormant minds
by the strength of Your presence.

We are forever leaving Egypt
    and returning.
Ordered journeys of birth and remembrance,
leading us back always
to the center where You are
our home and our freedom.

This Is Our Story Too

We know the story—
we read it every year
It is the story of how
a people, a small people enslaved in Egypt
were redeemed, released
with a mighty hand and an outstretched arm
Crossing through the mighty sea
walls of water on either side,
crossing from enslavement to freedom
from oppression to release.

But it is not just the story of our past,
of some distant ancestors—
b'chol dor vador, in each generation
we each are to see ourselves
as if we were personally redeemed from Egypt.

This is our story too—
For who among us has not been in Egypt
has not known her own "narrow places"
has not cried out bitterly?
Who among us has not wished for,
needed, perhaps still yearns for
redemption in her own life?

And who among us has not looked out
and seen that Egypt is not just metaphor
but the reality, the daily toil
of far too many
men and women, girls and boys.
That oppression continues
unabated, unchecked?

(continued)

47

This Passover, as we celebrate our ancestors' freedom
we remember our own narrow places
and we remember those
who are still in need of redemption.
At this season of redemption
we ask for our own release as well,
and we ask for the courage, the strength, the conviction
to work towards that better day
that day, as did our ancestors
we might yet sing
as they did
at the shores of the sea.

Fasting on *Tisha B'Av*, 5757

At sundown, I'm thinking,
Yeah, I can do this. Of course,
I've just pushed myself back
from a table of kugel and salad and
bread and then dessert.

At midnight, when I'm falling asleep to Letterman,
trying to think about what it means
to be a Jew today, with all these choices,
what these stories about a Temple
are trying to tell me,
my stomach starts to growl.

By noon the next day, I've spent
several hours thinking about the cracked
stained glass and stolen Torah scrolls.

My stomach yearns
for the irrational American belief
that it can't happen today.

My hair is greasy, my mouth
is dry, and my stomach is yelling
like the zealots at Masada.
Sundown finally comes,
and I remember last year on Yom Kippur
how I scarfed down chocolate
till I felt sick.
This year, I do it differently.

This year I sanctify my fast.
I say *kiddush*, and each sip is for the loneliness
I felt in the desecrated synagogue in Tsfat,
sacrificed just last year
because we dared to be female
and holding the Torah.
I say *hamotzi*, and each crumb
is a new Jew
born into a world
increasingly less hostile.

HONORING

OUR COVENANT

THE SHOAH

ISRAEL

THE SHOAH

The Nut Brown Sweater

Mamala, they took my things away from me.
May nineteen forty-two—my hair was long
and thick dark brown with waves that they quickly
cut all off. I was in my favorite nut brown
sweater jacket. They let me wear that as
I boarded the long black train to Auschwitz.

My mother, Cutla, came from Warsaw as
did my father, Herman. They put them on
a train that went to the crematorium—
there were so many I never knew which one.
And the children—we saw them board and we
knew then we would never see them again.

The number on my left arm? 13088.
You need a witness mister? I have none.
I have nobody. I am the only one
alive from the whole transport. No one else.
I went to Brooklyn, USA. Me and
My Abe. We married in Bergen-Belsen

then came here in 'forty-nine as tailors.
I was in my nut brown sweater jacket
and kept it with me 'til the day I died.
Julala, your hands go through all my things,
yet will they stop at this old brown sweater?
I'm here, your guiding hand, do not overlook.

Good, you see and cradle it in your arms.
You set it aside, not knowing why.
And then you find the framed photograph—
of me in that brown sweater with my long brown hair.
We knew then we were alone together.

Collections at Auschwitz

Glasses like weeds,
Frames tangled together
Like a little girl's hair.

Shoes like specks of dirt
Globbed into a sandcastle
At a beach without sunshine.

Suitcases,
Emptied like the ghettos
From which they came.
One name on each piece of luggage,
Each pile like a page in a phonebook
Of *Toldot Yisrael*.
The sacred generations of Israel.

Rolls of canvas,
Made of human hair.
Perhaps my grandmother's hair,
Or perhaps a little girl's.

I will carry this memory,
Like a heavy jug of water above my head,
From village to village.
Their stories are the water that sustains me,
Their memory, their glasses,
Their shoes, their hair.

Warsaw Ghetto, November 2008

Sometimes you have to look among the ashes to find a spark . . .

I went to the Ghetto looking for them.
Walking streets they also knew
like the back of their still unmarked arms.
But they were not these streets,
not these faces, not even like the ash
that rose from those chimneys.

I stood where the wall stood
to see what they saw,
but they were not there.

I found marble monuments
found their names etched in stone
but I did not find them.

I went to the Ghetto looking for them.
I stood on the ashes of
skeletal faces
empty eyes
orphan children
but they were not there.

Looking for them I went to the Ghetto.
I was on top of the bones of resistance
but it was not theirs.
I could see the *kindele*
climbing the wall, scampering for a scrap
but they were not them.

So I went to the cemetery
and I found white posts with black lines—
marking mass graves—but not theirs.

And then I sat in a park and held a corn poppy
as a black and white crow flew above me
I closed my eyes and found them.

Looking for them I went to the Ghetto.

Man Does Not Live by Bread Alone

As a child of four, my parents and I were hiding in the Greek
countryside to save ourselves from the Nazis. Fifty members
of our family were captured but by the grace of God and the
help of a righteous gentile, we escaped. We spent a year and
a half in the Greek mountains. Food was scarce and we were
hungry all the time. My father used to recite this passage from
Parashat Eikev, "Man does not live by bread alone, but with
whatever God can provide."

We were eating fruits and vegetables and drinking chamomile
tea. Water was available but not bread. Wild flowers of every
color, fruits, and the aroma of chamomile, sage, and oregano
compensated for the lack of bread. Everyday my parents
recited the *Birkat HaMazon* after our exotic consumption of
food. My parents' devotion to tradition kept our faith during
these difficult times. My parents were reassuring me that God
would send us some bread. A miracle happened, God provided us with bread. We recited the *Shehecheyanu, HaMotzi,*
and *Birkat HaMazon.*

It left a lasting grateful memory. I can hear my father's voice,
"Sarah, remember how we survived." "Yes Papa, by the grace
of God."

ISRAEL

A Prayer for Israel

May you be a light unto the nations, O Israel,
      Shining across the Universe.

We rejoice in Israel's beauty.
      Red mountains watch over lush fields.
Ancient temple walls echo the prayers
      Of countless generations.

We praise Israel's commitment to all who seek refuge
      In the land of our ancestors.
With joy and compassion,
      Israel welcomes the stranger.

We remember the brave souls who built our homeland.
      Their toil made the desert blossom and cities rise.
Just as Joshua and his flock labored in that Holy land,
      Our people continue to struggle, keeping Israel strong.

We thank God for the land of Israel, a precious gift.
We pray for God's blessing of peace, a precious gift.

Open a Gate for Us at the Closing of a Gate
A Prayer for Days of Political Disagreement in Israel

God of the breath of all life,
Grant us the courage to continue to right
The wrongs of the past
Even when pain is the price.
In order that our Land be a blessing
To all its inhabitants, its neighbors
And to all those who journey in this world.

Divine Presence, Source of all compassion
At the first flowering of the work of justice—
Protect the State of Israel,
the first flowering of our redemption,
the tapestry of life woven from a thousand hues and colors—
So that it will not unravel, so that it will not be torn asunder.
Keep a constant watch so that there will not arise among us
One who in sorrow would tear a hole in her.
Keep a constant watch so that there will not arise
one who would do her harm.

Our Father Our King,
Grant us strength during this time of Disengagement
to sew together the torn,
During this time of separation
not to cut down what has been planted,
When anger rages, grant us strength to embrace.
When we feel empty
help us to be inclusive and be included.
In Your light let us see light even when the skies are darkest
Answer us on the day we cry out to You.

Open for us a gate at the closing of a gate,
A pure heart and mind create for us, O God
And a spirit of rightness renew in our midst.

Standing at the Wall
An *Ahavah Rabbah* Prayer

How great Your love, oh God!
Embraced by prayer
Enfolded by a *tallit*
      The voices of my sisters wrap around me
          and raise me up
Standing at this Wall
Cleaving to Your mitzvot
      Cleaving to one another
          United in Your love
Oh, lead our hearts to understanding,
      Open our hearts to discerning
          Teach our hearts to listen,
That we might learn and teach
      Keep and do
          And establish You forever.
Through Your words and our deeds
Through Your Deed and our words.
Standing at this Wall
How great Your love, oh God!
You gave us commandments and covenant,
      Renewed each generation,
To guide us to Your dwelling place,
      Your sanctuary
          in each moment
Our mothers stood up, and entered
      Your sanctuary, Your dwelling place
That we might stand here
      Our sisters, our mothers,
Standing at this Wall
Do not be ashamed, do not be afraid!
Cling to the holy words
Dancing on ivory parchment

Down through generations
        Down from Eternity
                Dancing off the page
                        Dancing into the soul
We cling to those words,
        Let them lift us up
                to You
Standing at the Wall, we pray,
Gather us from the four corners of the earth, for peace
You gave us this wall for prayer, that we might know You.
You gave us this wall
        not to divide;
                To uphold
                        A bulwark that we might not tumble
                                A sanctuary ever in our midst

Gather us
        From the corners of our hearts
                For peace
Gather us
        And unite our hearts
                to unite Your name
Praised are You God, who in love chooses Your people Israel,
        To choose You
                To choose each other.
How great Your love, oh God!
Embraced by prayer
Enfolded by a *tallit*
        The voices of my sisters wrap around me
                and raise me up
Standing at this Wall

At the Wall

I stand in front of the wall and lift my hands, holding them an inch from the stone. I hesitate, not sure if I'm ready to touch it. This whole thing has felt sort of unreal to me until now. Even though I knew we were moving, as we packed and left Seattle, as our plane touched the desert ground, it all felt strange, as if my parents might turn around and say, "Just kidding Soph! You're not really going to spend your first year of high school in Israel—that would be crazy! It was a joke—we'll go home next week."

But here I am in front of this wall, and I'm strangely reluctant to touch it. This place is the center of Judaism; millions of Jews have worshiped here. For me to touch this wall right now would mean that I'm accepting those Jews as my people, and this place—this land—as my home for now. Slowly, I press my hands to the wall.

It's cool and smooth beneath my fingertips. I stare at my hands, touching. What was I afraid of? It's just a wall. And yet . . . I lift my gaze, let it travel up the ancient Jerusalem stone, and I look up at the sky, brilliantly azure. God, I'm not even sure if I believe in You, but if You're up there, and You can hear me, thanks. I kiss the wall, then turn and walk away without looking back.

Jerusalem

Where are you? Tonight
when I least expect you
your image flickers on TV,
and my last days
among your antiquities
loom up in the laundry.
Once more I lost my sense
of separateness from you;
I hear your oriental dissonance
peel away my western calm.
I feel your wars
tear into my dreams.
I eat your bittersweet fruit.

Jerusalem,
Let this hand
that writes
be silenced
if I forget you.

My Jerusalem

Entering—Re-entering
As though I never left.

All encompassing
Walking; seeing
Rooftops, land beyond.

City of Gold
Light changes
Bricks solid,
Building.

Feeling of Joy,
Presence of God.

Connecting to past,
Connecting to future.

God is present
Ir HaKodesh (The Holy City)

I AM HOME!

EMBRACING

OUR COVENANT

LIFE CYCLES

FAMILY

LIFE CYCLES

God-like

What does God look like? God looks like nothing. And nothing looks like God. But there are many things you cannot see. And still we are sure they are there.

~ Lawrence and Karen Kushner
from *Because Nothing Looks Like God*

This time,
these months,
before meeting the fetus in an ultrasound,
before finding out the sex,
it seems to exist mostly through faith.

Faith that those two pink lines on a stick mean
what I think they mean.
Faith in this being that I can't see, I can't hear, it's not a boy
or a girl to me yet,
it's simply existence and so much more.

A being with limitless promise, the very definition of potential.

I know it's there,
I'm certain,
but I can't touch it.
I speak, it listens—I know it listens—
but it doesn't respond.
It holds my words,
and my love,
and my feelings.

Existing inside of me, yet mostly intangible.

My unborn child,
10 weeks swimming,
has already taught me so much about
God, faith and possibility.

Prayer for the Birth of a Child

I hold your small hand and I plainly see
How very much I will love and care for thee.
I will teach you to be kind, loving and forgiving
And show you through my love the joy of living.
The years will pass by too quickly
And one day you will be grown
And pass what you have learned onto children of your own.
Keep me in your thoughts when we are apart
And always remember the love for you that is in my heart.

Prayers for Mothers Giving Birth

For a Baby Girl

Blessed are you God *[Yah]*
Mother of all living being
that out of me came new life in the world.
Blessed are you God *[Yah]*
whose wonders I now see and admire
deep are your thoughts.
Blessed are you God *[Yah]*
who guarded me during the past nine months.
Guard my newborn daughter
and be with her as you were with me.
Help me raise her in your ways.
Pour of your spirit on me and on her.
Spread your shelter of peace on her
for a good life and for peace
in health of body and soul.
Blessed are you God *[Yah]*
who kindly renews life in her world.

For a Baby Boy

Blessed are you God *[Yah]*
Mother of all living being
that out of me came new life in the world.
Blessed are you God *[Yah]*
whose wonders I now see and admire
deep are your thoughts.
Blessed are you God *[Yah]*
who guarded me during the past nine months.
Guard my newborn son
and be with him as you were with me.
Help me raise him in your ways.
Pour of your spirit on me and on him.
Spread your shelter of peace on him
for a good life and for peace
in health of body and soul.
Blessed are you God *[Yah]*
who kindly renews life in his world.

Growing a Grandmother's Heart

Of all the transitions a woman is blessed to experience, none may be as sacred, i.e., soul expansive, as becoming a grandmother. When she touches the baby for the first time, something new is born in her, a love so fierce and grateful it's almost embarrassing.

A grandchild has the potential to awaken the grandmother into her heart of wisdom because the child links her to another generation. She may remember her own grandparents with affection and now she knows from her own love for the grandchild how much she was once loved. The grandmother heart, known in wisdom traditions as the manifestation of unconditional love, is the grandmother's gift to the grandchild.

The grandchild births a more generous love in the grandmother. Perhaps for the first time, she cares not only about her own but for a generation in which she now has a vitally important rooting interest. She has lived long enough to know that we are interconnected.

Growing a grandmother's heart is neither gender nor age specific: it is a path of wisdom open to anyone who wants it. The grandmother embodies the archetype of lovingkindness. She is the good listener with a patience that gives you faith, and the unconditional love she offers becomes a teacher for you in the art of loving.

Daughter of the Covenant
A Bat Mitzvah Meditation

Envision your daughter as she lights the Shabbat candles for the first time. You sense the presence of your ancestors that came before you smiling upon your daughter—guarding her, supporting her. You see how her face glows as she draws the light closer to her with the movement of her hands. You see the mirror image of the candle flames reflected in her eyes. And as the room is filled with candle glow, you see a radiance emanating from your daughter of the covenant—an inner light, a light of the soul that merges and blends with the light of the candles. As you hear her voice chant the blessing, you sense the presence of angels in the light that fills the room. And, in this blessing, you hear another voice—perhaps the voice of an angel, perhaps the voice of the Shechinah.

Bar Mitzvah

A big weekend,
A special weekend,
Spent with a smile on my face,
Pride and joy, dancing
In my eyes
And tears, just below the surface;
Love, filling my heart,
Wrapping around me
In a way, that I can sense
Through every pore.
It fills the spaces
Where loneliness has lived.

So much living has occurred
In thirteen years,
Bar Mitzvah boys have no way
To know all the stories
Pages upon pages
Of stories surround him;
First in the pews,
Then at the tables
And on the dance floor.

Parents and grands,
Greats if they are lucky,
Sit beaming their love
And remembering with joy
And sadness;
Sweet times and sour,
Times spiced with cinnamon or pepper;
Sugar or lemon;
Times that just were.

Memories are long and fleeting
Some times moving like lightning flashes
Others lumbering like glaciers.

Bar Mitzvah boys
Know of the months of learning
Of memorizing and of planning,
Sunday school and Hebrew school,
Dream of presents and parties.

Parents remember births and first steps
And first words,
First days of school, loose teeth
Skinned knees, car pools, sports victories
and losses.
They hold their breath through prayer
recitals and Torah chanting
And wait with bated breath to hear
The secret speech;
Thinking of the details of the party
To follow.

This Grandmother remembers so much,
Of B'nai Mitzvah past,
Of babies grown to parents,
Of a family grown out of love
From two to many.
Sitting in the front row,
Photos from the past flash
Past as in a slide show,
While I hold tight to the moment
In great pride,
Wishing to freeze time.

Prayer for Our Graduating Seniors

G-D
We stand before you this evening with full hearts.
We look upon our children and we know
that we are coming to the close of a chapter in our lives.
For some, the beginnings have been joyful
For some, troubled.
For some, academic prowess has sustained them well
For some, heightened intuition and creativity
has blossomed.
Some will achieve their ambitions
Some will be disappointed and then find something more.
Some will enjoy social success
Some will be contemplative.

Some will always find hope
While others will confront despair.
Some will find love
And others will always seek the partner
of which they dream.
Some will pray for strength
And some will find their strength in deeds.
Some may never feel complete
While others will find serenity in study and in friendship.

We, as parent, families, and friends must soon release them
from our care and know that others now must guide them.
We will watch each journey with love and trepidation,
always anxious to prevent hurt,
and yet powerless to do just that.
Protect them G-D as they travel forth.
Grant them strength, courage and righteousness as they
continue on the path from whence we placed them with
faltering steps, strong hands and infinite, infinite love.

Grant that we be blessed to witness their adventures and their contributions to this glorious universe.

A Blessing for Students Going to Israel

A song of ascent, of David:
I rejoiced when they said to me:
Let us go up to the House of the Eternal
Now our feet are standing within the gates of Jerusalem.
(Psalm 122)

Our God and God of our ancestors, we thank you for the blessing of these young students. You have endowed them with wisdom and curiosity, courage and self-reliance, such that tonight they stand before You, ready to embark on an incredible journey. We ask for Your blessing as they go forth from our community to discover the land of our ancestors and learn from its people. Open their minds to new ideas, their ears to new languages, and their hearts to new experiences. Bless them as they walk through the land, and as they let the land walk through them. May the learning, prayer, and good works that they engage in bring light to their lives and to the lives of those around them. Surround them with the love of new friends and teachers, and when they need it, help them to remember the love of family, friends, and community that stretches across countries. And when the days of their journey have ended, bring them safely home into the arms of their loved ones.

There Are No Size 12 Shoes in the Hallway

There are no size 12 shoes in the hallway,
waiting to trip me today.
Tonight I won't lie awake listening for the sound of a door
shutting, a step on the stairs.
My kitchen will be as I left it tomorrow, not swarming with
dirty dishes and pans as if an army of elves altered it
overnight like some odd fairy tale.

My son has gone to college.

Help me, Oh God, to know that I wanted this. Walk with
me through this change in my life and in this relationship.

Help me, Eternal One, to let him learn from the bumps
and bruises of young adulthood, just as I let him learn
from childhood's skinned knees.

Walk with him, Oh God, through this transition in his life.
Help him to stand on his own two feet and help me,
Eternal One, to let him. Let him learn to go on alone as
he did when he learned to ride a bike, so that, now as
then, he will look at me and exclaim in stunned
amazement, "You let go!"

Help me, Oh God, to hear your words this fall
like never before:
> *To everything there is a season*
> *And a time to every purpose under heaven.*

Singing the *Sh'ma* for My Dad

My Dad planned his own funeral. While always a Jew in his heart and soul, my Dad was quite involved in Mom's church—sang in the choir, sat on the board.

When he asked me to sing the *Sh'ma* at his church funeral, I was quite honored, but it took a couple of days to say yes. I loved that it was so important to him and I was the only one of his children who *could* do this for him.

I sat with Dad many hours, chanting psalms and prayers, watching him very quickly fade away; singing the *Sh'ma* each time I thought he was taking his final breath.

On the day of his funeral, I was not sure I could actually sing in front of the huge crowd of mourners.

When the minister asked me to begin the service with the *Sh'ma* I was trembling. I closed my eyes and started singing the *Sh'ma*. Within seconds voices joined me—not just my husband and kids, not just *our* Jewish friends, but many voices, and it kept building. Jews scattered throughout the church all sang as one, the sacred words of our people that were still so important to my dear Dad.

That feeling of wholeness has stayed with me. I cherish the memory and look forward to each opportunity to sing the *Sh'ma*, connecting me forever to my Father, my Jewish roots, our people scattered throughout the world.

My Father's Arms

The left one
wore a watch well.

While his right one
held us crook-close.

Arms that tenderly
touched Nat's knee

taught Brian the art of
bait and tackle.

Arms that reached
intrepidly forward

saving war wounded
earning a bronze star.

And arms that shouldered
our shared burdens.

The Hyundai window
served as his arm rest.

Steer the wheel Dad.
Did you know

you were the force
behind our direction?

Did we thank you
for your tireless devotion?

Those slim, firm arms
full of purpose.

I miss them
more than sunlight

I kissed goodbye
My father's arms.

A *Yahrzeit* Prayer for Mother

Dear God and God of our Ancestors,

Grant my mother perfect rest.

She, like all humans, was complex in being. Celebrating her complexity as well as her simplicity rises in importance as my own years go by.

I give thanks for her life, which brought forth me, for her dedication to hearth and home, for her pursuit of kindness in her associations and for her ability to rise above loss and grief.

For the mysterious moments when she was difficult to understand, I am thankful for the gift of time, which washes away the rough edges of memory and brings forth the best of times.

How Long Is a Minute?

One minute, sixty seconds,
It can feel like forever,
Or just the flickering of a flame.

To a child, any child,
To be asked to wait
For a minute, they will feel
That it is like, eternity.

Minutes happen in all shapes
And forms,
At a red light it can feel, unending
Or when trying to apply lipstick
Or open a stick of gum,
It's disappeared.

So much can happen,
In a minute.
Life can begin,
One moment a child is not
And then like magic,
Magic, she takes her first breath
And begins the
march of minutes
That is her life.

Until, until, until
In an equally abrupt minute
Breathing stops
And there are no more
Minutes.

And when,
When you have experienced
Witnessed, visited with both,
You understand,
The unknowable,
That can happen
In a minute.

FAMILY

Loved One

He reaches to me
for rest, for comfort,
then lies languid
on the length
of my body.
His warmth seeps
into my cold.

I sing old songs
in the language
of my mother
and hers before,
"Schlaf mein kind"—
sleep my child.

Melody blends
with memory,
soothes away fear,
his and mine.
His small fingers
furl around my own
even in sleep.

As my hand goes numb
beneath his weight,
I try to leave.
He grips my hand
even tighter.
I surrender, stay.
I am grounded
forever as he
by love and history.

Perfection

As I walked in the light of the rising sun, I gazed upon the
beauty of the world;
I thought this must be perfection.
That evening the sunset's warmth comforted my soul with
peaceful bliss;
I thought this must be perfection.
Then during the dark, safe night my eyes were filled
with the innocent face of my sleeping child.
As my heart soared with a joyous love;
I thought here in the crib at the foot of my bed
is perfection.

Love Light

You ask, what is light?

I reply, which light?
Are you referring to the morning light,
       Those brilliant, waving shafts of daylight
       Which filter through a shutter's face?
If so, then I shall say,
Light is each day's blessing,
       A nurturing gift to all the plants and
       Animals that live upon this earth.

Or, are you asking about the evening light?
When we watch the sky's palette flow
       From jewel tone shades of amber
       To twilight's darkest mauve.
Of this I say, the beauty of evening light
Reminds us that the sun has moved
       To a place just beyond our view
       Where other children welcome a new day's light.

I wonder how "light" can be so "heavy" with meaning.
There are hi-lights, light meals, light operas, light hearts.
We turn on lamps for light.
Birds light on wires.
Helpmates lighten the load.
My mother tripped the light-fantastic.

We "see the light" when we reach
       New insights or understanding.
The *Ner Tamid* which illumines our sacred ark,
       Shows us the Eternal Light of Torah.

I've heard it said that the light we see
Begins in a place millions of miles above the earth.
    It crosses those miles in only one minute,
      To light upon us in a blush of warmth.
Of this I say to you, my precious child,
Look into my eyes,
      You will see a shining light.
      It is my love for you.

Michael, Age 6

He interrupts our Shabbas dinner
to taunt his sister into beating him.
Hours later, he runs to me eagerly,
happy to find an adult
who wants to see his basketball cards.
His *payos* curl down his cheekbones.
His eyes take up half his face.
He flips through basketball stats
while we bless the meal in our bellies.
He is the unity I have been trying to find.
I came here seeking simplicity:
Weeks of secular Friday nights
crashed into this first weekend in April,
the week before Pesach.
If anyone can free me from the slavery
of people whom I should let go,
of jobs that bring me down,
of thoughts that pound my brain,
it is Michael.

Shelter

We shelter the ones in our lives
Who require a helping hand,
a shoulder to lean on and arms to cry into.
We try and protect them from sadness, love lost,
illness and sorrows as best as we are able.

We shelter them because we love them,
and because they are in greater need than we are.
We give them brief sanctuary, because we care deeply
and to not do so would be against our nature,
and the Jewish imperative of helping others in need.

We know we cannot offer refuge from everything.
A broken heart needs time to be put right,
and some sorrows never really mend.
But a guiding hand is meant as a temporary respite
A time to come to terms with one's life.

During our lives we have received many types
of sheltering.
Mothers and Aunties, Sisters and Grandmothers
sheltered us from the many harsh realities of life.
They were there when we needed them most.
And now it is our turn to give safe haven
to the young and old of our families.

We give of ourselves and on occasion wonder
"Is it enough?"
And then as if by magic, our faith kicks in.
Whatever help we offer,
Whatever "shelter" we provide,
It is one less place that they will need to seek it out
elsewhere.

We are spiritually and culturally Jewish women,
Proud of it,
and dearly hoping our legacy lives on!

Growing Together

A little girl follows behind her mother who is planting
tulip bulbs in their garden. The mother is about three
bulbs ahead of her daughter. The girl's responsibility is to
pack the dirt on top of the bulb, except each time her
mother looks away—she pulls a bulb out. She thinks, "It's
lonely down there." So she puts three bulbs in one hole
together and packs it with dirt. "At least," she assures
herself, "they'll have company."

> So it is with us—as we uncover each bulb in our
> gardens, each story in our lives, we group them
> together for strength and comfort.

All winter long, the mother comes out to check on their
handiwork. And when in spring—every third hole sprouts
three shoots—she is perplexed. They so carefully tilled the
ground—what happened, she wonders?

> So it is with us—as we check regularly on our
> gardens—making sure things are growing
> according to plan.

In the end, for both mother and daughter, for us, there is
still growth. In ways we never expected.

Reflections on My Mother

As I brush my mother's hair, I reflect on our lives together and how they have changed. I have become her mother, and she has become my little girl.

When I was six, I would come home from school and say, "Mother, I'm home, where are you?" She was always there, asking about my day. I was sad when I got Mrs. Hand for my 5th grade teacher. Mother said, "It will be O.K." She was right. Mrs. Hand became my favorite teacher.

Mother was strong, stable and someone I could always depend upon. I called her first to tell her good news or bad news. Mother had few demands, but she insisted that I graduate college. And so I did.

When I became a flight attendant for Northwest Orient Airlines, we travelled throughout the world. I can still see her riding a horse in Petra, Jordan, and a donkey in Greece.

Six years ago, she moved from her house to an apartment for seniors. The roles reversed and I began to manage her life. As a child, she used to take me to medical and dental appointments. Now, I take her. She used to do my laundry, now I do hers. She paid my bills, now I pay hers.

When she phones me, I remind her to take her pills and to take walks in her building. Then, we can go to Las Vegas. "O.K.," she says.

Just as Mother was here for me, I am here for her.

How Have I Lived?

How have I lived?
Have I lived my days as a worthy bearer of Torah?

Was our home a sanctuary in which love
      And learning flourished?
Could you see in me a joyfulness
      As Sabbath Eve approached?

Did I rest my gaze upon you and listen with my heart
      As you confided youthful dreams or doubts?
When you sought my understanding did I hold you close,
      And with a tender kiss taste your silken tears?

Were you listening when I spoke to your grandparents?
      Were my words kind and gentle?
      Were they words of honor and respect?

Has my practice been truthful and disdainful of greed?
Have I shared my portion with those whose portions
      Were not full?

I pray that I have revealed our eternal connection
      To the words inscribed upon Sinai's ancient tablets.
And I pray that you have embraced those words.
      They are the treasures of our people.

May we remember the words of our heritage
      And think of them each day.
May wisdom replace youth's innocence.
Like Moses who delivered God's commandments to Israel,
      May we live our days as worthy bearers of Torah.

REFLECTING

ON OUR COVENANT

LIVING JEWISHLY

TALKING TO GOD

LIVING JEWISHLY

A Psalm to Friendship
An Acrostic

Adonai, You have given me a friend!
    Someone with whom to share life's journey
    We have made a covenant to:

Believe in each other,
    as we believe in You.

Care for each other's souls,
    as You care for them.

Depend on each other's counsel,
    as we weather life's storms.

Evil people will try to draw us apart
    But we will:

Fight for each other's ideals,
    or lose our own.

Guard against petty arguing,
    It accomplishes nothing.

How it can destroy!

Is friendship not the greatest gift we give to one another?

Joyously celebrate each other's accomplishments.

Keep jealousy reined in.

Love each other's fortes and flaws.

Make each day a new adventure.

Never take for granted
the feelings of your friend.

Open each other to new experiences,
Sharing the journey.

Promise not to pry, but . . .

Quietly console in times of pain.

Rejoice together,

Sharing in Simchas.

Trust in your relationship,
because it deserves your trust.

Understand your weaknesses,
Sharing your strengths.

Value your differences,
but delight in your common ground.

Walk together in God's presence,
Sharing the light of Torah.

Xenial always to each other and to our friends.

You and I will participate in Tikkun Olam.

Zealously we will appreciate our time together.

forever friends

forever friends
we are
how could we be
otherwise
so entwined
the stories
of our journeys
that they blur
at the edges
of whose good idea
or silly scheme
it was that sparked
this cherished moment
or that
now revisited
as we curl up
together in the big chair
warming our old bones
with the kindling of
memories
all the while
creating a cozy
haven to cradle
new dreams

kindred spirits
in each other's eyes
we see reflected back
our best selves
held sacred
heart to heart
protected from doubts
by the vigilance
of our shared love
and appreciation

chosen sisterfriends
leaning on each other
in the big chair
and in life
feeling our tenderness
toward each other
expand
to embrace the world

Sisterhood in a Splash
Standing at the Edge of the Mikveh

What brought you to this moment? Was it a class you took? Was it falling in love? Was it an earth-shattering revelation? Was it simply the feeling that this is the right path for you? Was it an invitation to attend services with a friend? Does your friend know the impact that this gesture made to your life?

What made you say "I need to do this"? Is there a relieved mother-in-law waiting in the wings? Is there a rabbi standing near who was your treasured guide on this spiritual journey?

Are you regretting every fattening food choice you've made for the last 25 years? Are you exposing the private bits that have remained safely tucked away from public view since high school gym showers—before time, pregnancy and gravity did their damage? No worries! It's your heart and mind that are the stars today.

(continued)

In a few minutes you'll be joining the "sisterhood" of all Jewish women. Some come regularly to the mikveh; others come as one important part of their conversion process; some will never experience this in their lifetime but their ancestors certainly did.

Every drop of liquid warmth welcomes you into this special sorority.

As you walk back up the stairs, shedding the softest water you've ever felt, all of the questions float away. There are only answers.

The most important answer is: I am a Jewish woman now.

My Mikveh Experience

I wanted to mark the very positive transition I felt upon reaching my 70th birthday. Just by chance, there was a workshop being offered at the mikveh at the Conservative Kibbutz, Hanaton, on the date of the 8th anniversary of my *aliyah*.

Never having been in a mikveh, I had been propelled toward this day by the new book, *Parashat HaMayim*, written by four Israeli Reform women rabbis. This book asks women to consider what Jewish rituals for women are relevant in the twenty-first century. My "way out" was to be that, if I were required to remove my nail polish, I could refuse!

The workshop began with a study of the concept of the mandala—concentric circles that call you to focus on their center, and are said to describe sacred spaces. I chose to go immediately into the mikveh before drawing a personal mandala . . . no way was I going to postpone this experience after I had come this far. And my nail polish was allowed to remain in place.

I walked into the warm water—the space dark around me, surrounded by glowing candles—and I immersed myself. No blessings were said, no one was observing me, I was alone and feeling very comfortable. I stayed down under the water for a rather long time, considering where I was and what I was doing and asking myself, "Why?" When I emerged, I thought about how many times I was going to dip. I considered 7 for 70 or 8 for *aliyah*. I chose 8, because I suddenly realized that I also have 8 grandchildren! Each time I immersed, I grew stronger and very happy that I was marking these two milestones in such a special way. I was taking time from the world of surrounding myself with others, and concentrating solely on me and my place in God's universe. I sought the center of my being, the center of my mandala. Suddenly, my mind envisioned the 8 turning on its side, and I felt the power of infinity. My core has infinite potential, my core reaches to infinity. I am alive and well and ready to take on new experiences.

My sense of awareness of everything around me centered only on myself, alone. I was ready to draw my mandala of 7s and 8s and infinity. And I felt immense joy. A joy that returns to me whenever I take the time to remember being in that place, in that water, in that calm.

She Leaves Nothing to Chance

I am a good girl, Mama.
Mama, I'm a good girl.

I look down on your tombstone.
The granite waits to receive you:
> Joanne Cullom Moore
> January 3, 1935 –

Across the marble march bronze medallions of your heritage:
> Huguenot Society
> Daughters of the American Revolution
> United Daughters of the Confederacy

"I prefer to not leave these things to chance," Mama sniffs,
standing next to me on tough Bermuda grass.
I am the chance she prefers to not leave this thing to.

"Look at your spot next to me;
you belong here, with your people."
I look down at my angry patch of sod,
permanently knitted to every other grave.

How many drops of blood does it take to make a people?
"One drop, but your bloodline is noble, proud and true.
Our family tree is pure—heroes all.
Look how far back we go."

Do your charts go back to Abraham and Sarah,
Isaac and Rebekah?
Can one drop ever be free of the millions that
precede and engulf it?
Can your Huguenot blood join with the blood of
the chosen people
Whom I've chosen?

Rabbi, will you bury me in a dusty Arkansas cotton field?
Mama knit the Bermuda just for me.
There are no stars on the gravestones there.
Only crosses.

I will come bury you, Rabbi says.
We will look up for our stars.
There are always stars above.

This is my heritage.
I am who I am.
You are not who I am.

Convert: A New Story

Sometimes the story must start from scratch
No matriarch to act as *shoresh*
You are both the root and the tender shoot
Then Shabbat is truly an act of creation

Threads of learning, guessing and your own emotions
Must be woven into whole cloth—
        both chuppah and challah cover
Sometimes fingers are clumsy
The fabric knots

No mother nodding assent, no guiding hands
Only you, to find the patience to untangle
Or the ingenuity to incorporate
And so you begin anew each week

Adding to your tradition, a tapestry of life

Must a Jewish Mother Be Jewish?

A mother is born before her child. Joy, responsibility, hope,
duty, dreams, terror. Boy or girl? Tall or short? Blonde or
brunette? Doctor or lawyer? Through what tradition shall my
child learn values? Celebrate milestones? Observe holidays?

And what of my agreement in the rabbi's office
so many years ago?
> Wanting to honor my partner.
> Wanting to honor my parents.
> Wanting to please my in-laws . . . is it even possible?

Raising a Jewish child. Where and how to start? Who to ask?
Who would know? What do I do and why?
> How should I know?
What is this holiday and why?
> How should I know?
What did you learn in religious school?
> How should I know?
If you don't know, how should I know?

A new way.
What if?
What if we change our words and thoughts: children do not
marry out, they marry who they love?
What if we stop grieving our loss, rending our clothes?
What if we demonstrate, by our own observance and actions,
the beauty and meaning in Judaism?
What if we invite the loving stranger to share, to learn,
to experience, to discover?
What if we honor and respect the loving stranger's tradition?
What if the loving stranger embraces our tradition?
What if the loving stranger takes this journey with us?
And what if we answer why Judaism for ourselves?
A new way.

Have Patience, Dear Sister

Have patience, Dear Sister

This time in your life is a transition
and a bit of a challenge
and not where you want to be

> *maybe not for the same reason, but I have been there too*
> *and so have your sisters*
> *we know*

It is not a comfortable place
not a comfortable feeling
and not where you want to be

You feel like you are in limbo
out of sorts
out of control

> *maybe not for the same reason, but I have been there too*
> *and so have your sisters*
> *we know*

But as soon as you embrace this time as the blessing that it is,
You will be guarded by angels
some you know
more that you do not know
and always, always by God!

> *you can count on that . . . I know*
> *and so do your sisters*
> *we know*

Have patience, Dear Sister
Know that you are not alone!

> *you can count on that . . . I know*
> *and so do your sisters*
> *we know*

what might you be willing

what might you be willing
to let stay
unresolved
incomplete unfixed?

what burden could you
lay down by the side
of the road
and ease forward
without ever looking back?

what last straw would you
leave unturned and unexamined
in order to lighten your load
enough to soar on the winds
of something as simple
and satisfying as
unimpeded joy?

what might you allow
to go unlisted
undated undone
so as to release the tethers
holding you fixed
and anchored to obligations
that have chosen
and been chosen by
you?

what could you relinquish and
what price would you gladly pay
for the precious privilege
of quiet contentment
and could you
without regrets
leave furled the flag
of endless achievements
in order to surrender to
the holy sweetness of
unencumbered being?

Soaking in Torah

We are commanded—*laasok b'divrei Torah*—to engage in
the words of our Torah.
We are commanded—*laasok b'divrei Torah*—to immerse
ourselves in the story of our people.
We are commanded—*laasok*—to soak ourselves, jump in,
dive in, make a big splash.
B'divrei Torah—in the words of our people.

Savor each letter—as it drips with honey,
sweet in our mouths.

Thank You, *Shechinah*

Thank You, *Shechinah*, for making me who I am today, and for guiding me to become the kind of person I strive to be.

Thank You for my eyes, so that I can see, and for inspiring me to look for the Divine Spark in others.

Thank You for my ears, so that I can hear, and for teaching me how to listen.

Thank You for my hands, so that I can touch, and for expecting me to reach out to others.

Thank You for my mouth, so that I can talk, and for challenging me to speak up for those who are not able to speak for themselves.

Thank You for my feet, so that I can walk, and for urging me to march for just causes.

Thank You for my heart, so that I can love, and for helping me to feel the love and pain of others.

Thank You for my shoulders, so that I can stand tall, and for encouraging me to offer a shoulder for others to lean on.

It has been said that people might forget what you said or what you did, but they will never forget how you made them feel.

Please help me, *Shechinah*, to be caring, feeling, loving, mindful, and attentive, and to always be present for those who may need me.

A Jewish Legacy

I've been called a bleeding heart

In silence I bear the sadness
For every story of oppression
That has reached my ears
From long ago in time of Moses
Through recent histories of those who perish
And suffer unspeakable indignities
During too many holocausts of hate

My heart wrenches at reminders
That injustices exist in faraway lands
Genocide in Darfur, famine in Somalia
While over-indulgence and obesity threaten
The children of our nation
With our guilt we feed their bodies
With our guilt we starve their spirits

In despair I watch
The hardening of hearts
As disasters fade with yesterday's news
And violence rises as a city's statistic
And earth mourns its decline of health
When rules are kept and laws are made
To exclude those who already have so little

I have been called a bleeding heart
In my collective memory
I remember my ancestors' plight
How they struggled to be free
I carry within me this gift of conscience
God has bestowed upon my soul
I am a bleeding heart—
I am a Jew!

To Life

In an old bookstore on Georgia Avenue,
I walk gingerly through the dusty stacks,
touch gold-embossed, leather spines
of holy books, of ancient texts,
as though they are my ex-husband's skin.
A man repairs a tallit's fringes,
wrapping tzitzit in deft certainty,
the blue thread luminescent.
Velvet or wool, crocheted kippot
lie stacked in plastic bins.
I look at fancy wedding cards,
at plaques whose household blessings
wish me and mine safe haven.
I lift glasses to shatter under the chuppah.
Silver Shabbat candlesticks light the sweet
promise of home, remind me
to keep my vows, to keep the peace.
I stand a moment. My eyes fill with tears.

The shop owners, a man and woman
more than fifty years united, call to each
other above the cash register's hum.
In her wig and long skirt, she meets him
near the shelves of kosher cookbooks.
She caresses his dark suit's lapels,
straightens his tie and whispers in his ear.
She needs something from the back room.
He looks me over, nods and disappears.
He brings it on the run, hands it to her, smiles.
She winks at him and turns to me, her customer.
I ask for a book on marriage and a copy
of the Talmud, a treatise on oral law, on how to live.

I ring up my purchases and thank her.
In the car, I open the bag and search
for the receipt. There, at the bottom,
wrapped in blue and white tissue,
I find a filigree chai, a golden chain.

Arvit (Evening Prayer)

Leave him alone, I say to the girl
as if it were the most natural thing
in a city like New York.
Leave him alone, I say with great calm,
authority and love, love for the stranger
I suddenly notice, a man to himself
amid the leisurely evening crowd. Not
a Hasid outwardly, just a plain-clothed
Jew, he stands near his cart, swaying
in that familiar, fervent motion
I recognize.

I don't know where the North is,
but I know he is facing East, Zion,
where, in the early dawn, my father
laps the thin *T'fillin* straps
over his arm, binding himself
to God, the small scripture box
extending from his forehead.
He thinks I am
deep in the sleep

(*continued*)

he led me to the night before
when he lifted me up
to kiss the *mezuzah*,
ask for my breath
to come back in the morning,
and no nightmares please Oh
God all-merciful.

Leave him alone, I say to the girl,
and she whispers, I'm sorry, runs
to join her friends. She wanted to buy
a hot dog, and in her young, impatient voice
called out to the vendor, Hey sir, hey mister.

Leave him alone, I say to the girl,
he is praying.

Just Be Nice

Our congregation has a good many older folks, and as a result,
we are losing them far too frequently. But even in their
passing, they are teaching us how to live. At the funeral of one
of our dear, gentle ladies, many good things were said about her
and how she lived. But one thing has remained with me since
that day several years ago. One of her children said that she
was known for telling them, when they were complaining or
criticizing or just fussing, to "Be nice. Just be nice." To me, this is
a big life lesson in just a few words, and I shall always remember
her for the advice she gave her children. How much better this
world would be if everyone would just be nice.

Jewish Girl's Guide to Guacamole

The avocados must be chosen carefully,
firm to the touch but supple like a baby's
tochis. Peel the thin skin tenderly
before mashing the dense green fruit. Stir in
the red bite of salsa infused with chili peppers,
cumin, garlic, a bissel salt. Then squeeze
the clear yellow of lemon over the mishmash.

These colors are strangers
to the complexion of Jewish foods—
variegated browns of brisket and kishkeh,
umber of chopped liver, bronzed beige
of blintzes, crisped copper of potato latkes,
dusted tan of kreplach, k'naidlech, k'nishes;
translucent gold of chicken soup and matzoh balls.

These foods, the cast of autumnal earth,
of soil and sand and dirt, of land we lived off
but could never own, we put into our mouths
that we may grow roots into our migratory lives.
Refugees, we chew quickly, our cheeks
streaked with grease, to taste
the mineral pigments before they dissipate.

These foods are cooked slow,
the longer the better—
boiled, baked, roasted, simmered, stewed,
until they wrinkle, wither, fold, implode,
the exact time and temperature
no matter, as if heat could burn
the bitterness from our repast.

we are none of us wise enough alone

considering that we are
none of us wise enough
or strong enough or clever
or creative enough alone
how considerate and necessary
it is that we remember
time and again to turn to one another
with gratitude and respect

considering the ways that we are
each of us so interdependent
on one and another
our lives so interwoven
down to the details and intricacies of
our every day goings and doings
that something as simple
as putting food on our table
or even simply setting a place
or more simply still
seeding a garden or field
requires the work and wisdom
of thousands of hands and tools
and practices that stretch back
to the beginnings of time
even to the harnessing of fire
the weaving of baskets
and the discovery of the wheel

while we as humans have collectively
scaled the highest peaks and soared
way into the heavens
reached far into the depths
of oceans and delved into the magnificent

complexities of our own bodies
and minds not one of us
could have done any such thing
on our own

and so it is that we must truly be
forever and always beholden
beyond measure to those
upon whose shoulders we stand
those who came before and those
who journey with us now

and what is ours to do in this
and every moment
with great humility
and even greater awe
is quite simply to remember
and give thanks

TALKING TO GOD

Noah's Wife Talks Back

I don't know what he was thinking.
He comes home one evening,
announces we have to pack up all our belongings,
all our animals, all our family
build an ark.

He said God spoke to him
I said, *Why now?*
The world has gotten dark
The world has fallen into violence
The world has succumbed to hatred and fear.
I said, *It has been that way for years*
So why now?

Why give up now?
Why walk out on the world,
Why destroy everything
rather than start the hard work
trying to repair it?

He didn't listen.
They never listen, these men.
They build, they argue, they fight.
They destroy and argue some more.
Then they take their toys and go home.
I don't know whether I'm talking about God
or my husband.
Some days
they're indistinguishable.

In the end, God came around
to seeing it my way:

As soon as the flood waters receded
as soon as the earth dried
as soon as the rainbow appeared
God pledged never to do it again.
But it was too late
for my neighbors, my friends, my city.
Wayward and disturbed perhaps
it was my home.

Creation Prayer

Mysteriously, God created the universe,

with all the laws and marvels that scientists study:

gravity, evolution, physics, fire, birds flying,

caterpillars turning into butterflies,

the workings of the human mind;

but God's greatest creation is

the ability to love and to be loved.

Mi Chamochah

You brought me out
From the narrow constraints of my self-loathing,
Extended your hand to me
B'yad chazakah u'vizroa n'tuyah
A strong embrace,
protective and warm
Like my mother's arms.

Your tender voice,
Speaking to me from within a flower,
A rosebush with thorns afire,
Assuring me that I can make more of this life,
That I don't have to stay
In this cage,
Oppressed, alone, enslaved to this pharaoh.

You have reignited the passion within me.
My soul now thirsts for You.
I cannot wait any longer!

You promised to save me long ago,
Before I could ever promise
That I'd be worth redeeming.

Thought for the Day

This morning I found myself humming Debbie Friedman's version of the prayer, *Elohai*: "*Elohai, Elohai, n'shamah shenatata bi, t'hora hi.*" "*Elohai,* the soul that You have given me is pure." I love the idea in this prayer—so different from the Christian doctrine of original sin—that we are, in our deepest essence, pure: whole and just as we were meant to be. But this morning, humming along, it struck me that because the word *n'shamah*, "soul," is grammatically feminine, the prayer literally says, "*Elohai,* the soul that You have given me, *she* is pure." My deepest self, not just as a person, but as a woman—*she* is pure.

So often the Torah assigns particular impurity to women. Even the blessing of giving birth renders a woman "unclean;" forbidden from touching anything holy, she passes on her impurity like so many cooties to everyone and everything she touches. So often a woman is impure simply by virtue of being a woman. But by a happy coincidence of grammar, the Hebrew word for "soul" is "feminine," allowing me to use this prayer to give thanks that my soul—the feminine implanted within me—is an expression of divine wisdom and purity.

Small Voices

Shall I rant and rave
about the injustices that surround me?
Will you hear my voice if it is LOUD?
As a woman, as a mother, I find myself better heard
if I speak
in a small voice.
I fight my inclination to assume you hear me better if I yell.
All you will hear is the din and
I, in the process, will deafen myself and
I, in turn, will no longer hear.
The voice is a beautiful instrument if played correctly.
The voice is a powerful instrument if played quietly.

Hear me—*Sh'ma.*

Hear the still small voice within yourself.
Hear the still small voice within each other.
A sea of voices speaking quietly,
as Hannah did so many years ago.
Our voices.
One voice.
Then perhaps You will hear me.

Be a *Sukka* to Me (*or* A Jewish Matryoshka)

Be a *sukka* to me, be shade, be space, light and dark, and paper lantern, made by the children at the nursery.

Be foliage to me, be *s'khakh*, be fresh: grass beneath, branches above. Be the whisper of breezes, be small insects hovering.

Be sheets spread out, be careless, be an old stain that would not come out in the wash, be a picture hung a little off center, the ends of a paper chain from last year.

Be a *sukka* to me in the desert, a shepherd's shack by his flock, be shield and protection to me (not wall, or tower, or fortress, or cloister).

Be memories that never were to me, and countless forgettings. Be new to me, be Ancient of Days.

Be the beating of hearts, a slight lowering of the head upon entering, be a nod of greeting, and the laying down of cake or pie on a low table.

Be the funny bending of a branch or hanging fruit, harmless laughter, a conversation from the *sukka* next door, which comes like a river flowing.

Be the image of my loved ones to me, a little different in the dimming light.

Be a *sukka* to me, and within it, like a spacious Russian doll, I shall be a *sukka* to those I love.

A Reflection on Holiness

Working as a chaplain in a county jail is challenging. It is a cold, concrete place—a dark and dreary place. But it is not without light. The light does not come from the sun, but from the souls of the men and women inside who recognize there is a different way. When I would sit and talk with them, I saw the faces of real people struggling, and could see their light. The jail became a place of holiness. I understood that, like myself, they were made in God's image and were, therefore, holy. They made mistakes—sometimes very large ones—but the spark of God still resided within them. The Hebrew word for holiness is *kedushah*. One of its meanings is "set apart." Los Angeles County Jail was a place set apart from the rest of society, people perceived as being "separate." One way to understand this separateness was as a world cast aside, full of people who did not deserve our attention. Yet, I saw and experienced something else. I saw a place in which people who were cast aside became set aside . . . people who—through the help of sacred text, prayer, and community—connected to their own innate *kedushah*, and created a space of *kedushah* for others. After only a short time there, I could say "God is surely present in this place, even if I did not at first know it."

Zusha at Lake Tahoe

Why can't I be like You?
Zusha asks God.
God answers:
Board a boat
to the Reed Sea.
Better yet, this lake—now.
This lake? Now?
Don't ask questions. GO!

So I board a boat, stare
into dark water and over it,
inside my head and out—
beyond the Sierra.

Light comes to me,
and fills me. I gather in
this lake and this mountain range
becoming for a moment not God,
but at last my own true self.

Listen, My Soul, Listen

Sh'ma Yisrael, Adonai Eloheinu, Adonai Echad.
Listen, my soul, listen.
Listen to the voice of God in the wind and the waves.
Listen to the whisper of our ancestors
As they danced to freedom on that ancient shore.
Listen, my soul, listen.
Listen and feel.
Feel the hand of God move through you,
Feel the footsteps of our ancestors
As they danced to Miriam's timbrel.
Sh'ma Yisrael, Adonai Eloheinu, Adonai Echad.

Asher Yatzar

As magazine pages flutter in the breeze,
Glossy, thin sheets whisper cruelly:
Your body is disgusting,
You have too much fat, too much hair.
Your teeth are not white enough.
Your nose is too big.
You will never find love.

But I know better, and I have found love.
I am worthy. I am grateful.
I am thankful for this body, this magnificent vessel
    that You have given me.
Its complexity, still greater than
    the most advanced electronic device.
Millions of molecules, just doing their thing.
Like clockwork, my breathing in and out,

Limbs enabling me to traverse this universe,
So perfect, and yet unnoticed until something goes wrong.

How could I forget to cherish this body, O God?
With its miraculous innards and exterior that
You fashioned with love.

Baruch atah, Adonai, rofei chol basar umafli la'asot.

How Can I Ask?

How can I ask
For clarity and truth
For what is needed most in the world
When so much in the world
Is broken?
How can I reconcile
Needing
When so many are in need?
I feel powerless
To fix, to heal and repair
And yet
My prayers
Help heal
What is broken
In me
So that I may do
For others
And in a way
That is everything.

Oneness

When our people
Was called
To listen
We heard the Voice
Of the Eternal
Speaking in our hearts
To believe
In what we could not see
To hope
In what we could not touch
And thus
We found the courage
To know that You exist.
In us,
In others,
In nature,
In spirit,
Seen and unseen
Tangible and intangible
Unifying
Oneness.

A Meditation on *Ma'ariv Aravim*

When You divided the day from the night,
You opened the gates to living divisions:
separating the sea from the land, species from species
all the creatures that roam the sacred Earth.

Something of You is threaded
in our ever-dividing cells—and so we learned
to separate one sound from another,
into words and language, understanding
Your divisions between good and evil.

Perhaps then You were no longer lonely,
for a conversation began between us
that continued through millennia
and will expand, like Jacob's ladder,
to the stars, and to the inmost recesses of our being.
For You are the Eternal One, the Creative Divider,
the Presence whose speech brings forth life and love.

I Wonder With Wonder

Words of hope, of inward peace
Silent, or whispered as a soft wind blows
Quiet and careful, mellow and sweet . . .
I wonder with wonder where my prayer goes.

Words of thankfulness and gratitude
Chanted in song, with harmonious care
Resonant, passionate, open and pure
I wonder with wonder who hears my prayer.

Words of sorrow, adversity, pain
Crumbling dreams, oppression and fear
Desperate and tearful, imploring and crude
I wonder with wonder, can anyone hear?

Words of wisdom, conviction, faith
Conscious awareness, a sense of bequest
Embracing our circumstances, the good and the bad
I wonder with wonder, am I doing my best?

Words of engagement, care and grace
Moved to action for others' needs
Selfless charity, service and love
I wonder with wonder, my words are the seeds . . .
I wonder with wonder, the wonder of deeds.

DRAWING STRENGTH

FROM OUR COVENANT

LEGACIES

SEEKING HEALING

LEGACIES

Sh 'ma

Shhh . . . listen.

Shhh . . . you have to listen to hear.

Shhh . . . can you hear?

. . . can you hear the surprise and delight in Sarah's laughter?

. . . can you hear the joy and pride in Miriam's song?

. . . can you hear the strength and wisdom in Deborah's clear judgments?

. . . can you hear warmth in your grandmother's voice calling you to the Shabbos table?

. . . can you hear your mother's love as she recites the Sabbath blessings?

. . . can you hear your daughter's clear, high voice chanting as she joins the circle of women?

. . . can you hear your sisters' earnest prayers as they share their goodness and courage?

. . . can you hear your granddaughter's newborn cry as she joins the Jewish chorus?

. . . can you hear your own heart beating, reaching to join the song of praise for Adonai?

Shhh . . . can you hear?

. . . can you hear the women who came before you?

. . . can you hear the women yet to come?

. . . can you hear us all as one?

Shhh . . . listen . . . hear . . .

Sh'ma . . .

Avot v'lmahot, A Prayer of My Legacy

My Jewish Soul remembers
My father, Abraham, off to morning minyan
To say *Kaddish* for his father Jacob
Who died when I was four

My Sabbath Soul of memories
Holds my mother Lillian's image lighting Shabbos candles
Reciting the prayer of words she only understood in meaning
A Blessing from her mother Dora—my namesake

Elohai, in Your Greatness and Compassion
You've known my ancestors who've followed Your Path
Some steadfast in their rituals, others steadfast in their deeds
All who have sought Your Lovingkindness and Embrace

Adonai, count me among them in Your Presence,
In the generations of loved ones before me
And in those who will follow
Linked in the chain of sacred transition
Forever comforted in Your Shelter and protected by Your Shield

On Giving Thanks

Although I grew up in a traditional Jewish household, being Jewish was not a particularly positive experience. Danger lurked everywhere.

In Europe, Hitler was murdering our cousins. At home, anti-Semitism seeped through the floorboards of the local schools. Unlike my parents, who grew up shouting Yiddish on the Lower East Side, we in Queens were warned to be quiet.

Our neighborhood was full of churches. After the war, a Conservative synagogue—as grand as any of the churches—was built. My parents sent me to Hebrew school, where I was confirmed in 1948.

The birth of the State of Israel provided a new definition of Judaism. Drawn to Zionism, I lived and worked in Israel for a while. Returning to New York, it was easy to preserve the rituals of Judaism without spiritual involvement.

Everything changed when the first of my four granddaughters was born. Experiencing the continuity of life has awakened in me a sense of gratitude that is overwhelming. Judaism, for me, has become an expression of gratitude. Little wonder that nearly all our prayers are blessings. We thank God for the creation of the sun and for the privilege of learning Torah.

My prayers today are simple. I am grateful, first, for the lives of my children and grandchildren; second, for the love of Judaism they share; and last, I thank God for the gift of life and for allowing me to celebrate this new season.

The Flow of Generations

The old order changes,
Generations come and go.

A little child stands on tiptoe,
How does it work? She asks.
Mother shows.

A young person sits at a desk,
The machine before him,
He knows the way to go.

A new immigrant comes home from school,
She tries her new language
As the parents listen.
Two grandparents applaud
Though they do not understand.

An older person sits together
With friends.
As they talk, the machine before them
Is silent.

The old order changes,
Generations come and go.
Youth know all answers quickly,
Older wisdom is slow.
Generations support each other
As they grow.

Pardes: My Neighbor's Garden

 Peshat

A map of the garden:
In the center of the garden, a downed tree
and a deck where the tree stood
In the southwest, a swing set with a slide and tower
In the northeast, a cord of firewood neatly stacked
To the north, a blue pool
In the south, a massive evergreen
Southeast, climbing bittersweet
Surrounding all, a wooden fence.

 Remez

A child lives here
who never swings or climbs the tower
Sometimes we hear
mute animal cries
occasionally tears,
more often, the father's saw, hammer, drill
Evergreen branches overspread the fence
almost to our roof.
We share the birds.

Derash

The swing set with the tower signifies hope unfulfilled
The deck suggests man rising above the dust
The firewood is the downed tree transformed
In the blue water is healing and pleasure
The evergreen laughs at the illusion of fence:
        My garden and his grow together
The birds imply we are to feed each other
The bittersweet is menace springing alarmingly among my mint
The fence is a circle drawn around the heart
The child is all its tender, broken care
The father's skill is love.

 Sod

Every garden holds a secret
whose meaning we may read
in wet branches through fog
bird tracks in snow
in the scars and calluses that shatter and reroute
the heartline of the gardener's rough palm.

Torah Romance

My righteous lover stands before the Ark
hugging me, Torah, to his yearning chest.
A diminutive leader of great stature and charm,
the rabbi raises my five books high, adoring my text.

I stand upon the bimah in his steady arms
dressed in my blue mantle of fine linen and silk.
Encircling my throat, the silver necklace of the yad,
haloing my head, gold and pearl crowns, honey and milk.

He dances, me, his princess, down the narrow aisle
three times around the sanctuary for good luck.
Friends and family reach out to touch my soul
and kiss me with the lips of their prayer books.

He carries me over the lectern's threshold,
lifts the heavy robe above my thin sheep's skin,
tenderly unfolds my fragile parchment scrolls
baring my storied melodies of goodness and sin.

I feel the weighty pointer tickling my spine.
Its fingers trace graceful arches of Hebrew figures.
Characters sway and daven across the line,
celebrate the invincibility of ancient scriptures.

From Czechoslovakia, I am the Brno Torah,
sole surviving remnant of that 600-year-old ghetto
obliterated in the bonfires and tears of HaShoah.
I remain the only witness to Brno's last libretto.

Inside me still live all the words of the universe.
No wisdom left unsaid by letters of the aleph-bet.
All my meanings await to be deciphered and discerned.
I carry my progeny in rapture, precious seeds of my flesh.

Reasons and Voices

Echoing across the bimah I hear the voices silently
seeking the reasons
for the journey we are on.

One recalls a childhood opportunity not offered.
Another remembers a lack of motivation as a child
and then the years
swiftly slipping by and now just seemed like the right time.

For others it is not so much a completion of a goal
but a continued commitment
to Judaism and the growth and desire to learn
how our lives are meant to be lived,
and excitement of what will come next.

One voice says that to learn the language of her ancestors
and to be able to pray as they did
brings her closer to her faith.

Yet another voice floats by saying that it was
to continuing healing, for seeking courage
and having a family to belong to.

For some, there were no words that could express what
they felt in their hearts.

Our journey is like the Tree of Life. Its trunk sustains us,
its leaves and branches, ever growing and changing.
And as we study and learn, we can fulfill
the promise of *L'dor Vador*
and keep Judaism alive
for those who will follow us.

Peaches, Netanya, 1970

He sold peaches from his cart
Avram, an old immigrant
from Eastern Europe, paler
than I, light eyes and lashes.

I never knew if he landed here
before or after the war
when he might have
shortened his name.

With him was his helper, young
Yosef the singing Yemenite;
his dark sandaled feet dangled
over the cart pulled by a donkey.

They slowly rolled into
our village just before
the arrival of noon heat.

Cush, the dog, ran along side
of them. He knew his way back
to nearby borders and the sea.
He always licked my face.
They both knew I'd buy; I always did.
We went through our dance:
"What do you call that?"
I pointed to a peach.

"*Ahfarsek*," Yosef pronounced
the word with gutteral sounds.
Odd word, I thought, copying
the way he placed his tongue

against the roof of his mouth,
repeating, "*Ahfarsek*."

"Excellent! Now taste!" he laughed.
The older man, silent as always,
sliced the soft fuzzy skin.
"Sweet, yes?" Yosef grinned.

"And here, Madame, apples of the earth
Mish-mish. Here is the best.
Better here than in our cities."

Oh, fruit of the land
Oh, milk and honey.
Where are you now,
singing Yosef,
silent Avram,
lost Cush.

two crones

my grandmother
was a modern woman
left the old country
and the old ways
behind and taught me
to play gin rummy
and go fish
and to sew pretty clothes
for my fancy dolls
she laughed a lot
and loved life
and had no patience
for regrets

my bubbe
was an ancient woman
of another time
and another place
a reluctant refugee
who sang old songs
with strange words
and taught me
to bake mandelbread
to light candles
and to sip tea
with sugar cubes
on my tongue

ah sweet childhood
memories
how I was blessed
beyond measure

to be loved and cared for
by these two crones
from one I came
to understand
the promise
of the future
from the other
the sacredness
of the past

The Number Three

Three sisters
Three Matzah Covers for our Seder tables
Three Chanukiyahs; all like Mom's
Connections across time and space
Traditions passed from Mother to Daughters
Tears and smiles
Three unfinished identical needlepoints
Found in a drawer after the funeral
Working together to finish them was an easy choice
Not an easy task
The oldest cries as she makes each stitch
The middle daughter cannot pick up the canvas
And the youngest cries as she makes each stitch
Connections to our Mother's love
On our holiday tables and in our hands and hearts
Memories and love
Three Sisters saying *Kaddish*

Low Country Jewess Comes of Age
and Confronts History

I knew as soon as I walked up the block
gefilte fish boiled in my mother's steaming kitchen.
The stench of fish heads, onions, limp celery
overpowered me. I wanted to run.
Mama stood over the stove,
grey stained apron flapping
in the April breeze.
Sweat beaded on her forehead
as she shaved carrots for curling
in iced water.

On the porch draped with wisteria,
the maid grated horseradish.
Its nostril-burning strength
made her throw back her head
and wipe her cheek on her shoulder.
Azaleas peeked over the rail
swooning in the southern spring.
Matzo crumbs, ubiquitous as
beach sand, gritted the floor.

I stepped inside the new, old country.
Eastern Europe emigrated
to East Carolina at least once a year.
My annual task waited for me—
to make the charoset.
The red pile of cinnamon grated,
pecans chopped, and apples sliced,
I had only to mix them with a cup
of cough-syrup-sweet wine
into a symbol,
of ancestral slavery.

Ode to Chicken Soup

There is—YECCHH—store-bought chicken soup.

There is restaurant—YECCHH YECCHH—chicken soup.

But the Best Chicken Soup

Is Homemade . . .

My Mother's Chicken Soup.

Sometimes chicken soup reminds me of the Caribbean Sea.
It's clear enough to see the bottom
The parsley waves, unanchored like floating green leaves
    of seaweed.
The matzoh ball is the reef looming large,
    hopefully yielding and
Not rock-hard to founder on.

There is no scientific formula for chicken soup.
It is a marvel of genetic engineering
From grandmother, to mother to daughter,
    generation after generation.

Some of us have tried to teach sons
    how to make chicken soup
But it seems it is truly resistant to
    the extra Y chromosome.

Shalom Haverah (Friend)

Despair,
it seizes me,
my soul longs
to see your face
here
in the moment,
face-to-face,
touchable,
alive.

Your face
in treasured
memoried photos.
Your face
telling lifetime stories,
sparkling, smiling—
serious, contemplative—
attentive, introspective—
elusive & enigmatic—
all storied faces
some I had almost forgotten.

Your voice,
hearing
your gentle, sweet voice
speaking. Quietly.

Your voice,
closer
in your letters
tucked away, neatly folded
in this gold leaf-adorned
box (your gift to me)

carefully
secured under lock & key.

Your face,
Your voice,
So many reminders of you
of how it used to be
for us . . . then.

Phone talk, occasionally
'til 2 AM
when sleepiness halted
our girlish laughter—
later replaced by wife,
mother, grandmother
chats
Sharing joys and sorrows,
sharing
a lifetime of trust.
Agreeing
always to be together.

Then
Your face without motion
Your voice without breath
Your heart without beat
My heart
cried out in despair,
my pain unstoppable.

Now
Standing here,
prayer book in hand,
for morning minyan
davening (praying) with others

(continued)

saying *Kaddish* for you
as the sun seeps
into the shul's stained-glass
windows, sparkling,
the only bright light
in my endless darkness—
and I weep.

Joining others' afflicted souls,
hearts broken, all
struggling in pain
uttering the *Kaddish* prayer
collective voices
join,
affirming life,
my life
so empty now.

A part of me has died
with you,
never to be restored.

Someday I will join you.

Shalom Haverah.

Ancestral Voices

My Californian Sukkah down below
is filled with youthful voices,
while I up here watch shimmering olive leaves and lie
basking in diaspora sun
reading about my grandfathers:
prisoners of the Pale, the pious,
Kabbalists, Maskilim, Bundists,
Capitalists, Zionists, dreamers,
Kibbutzniks, fighters, well-diggers,
wishful-thinkers.

My sons and daughters downstairs with their eager voices
Approach my impasse as I must have done,
As once my grandparents set their sights on Zion,
Forsaking history and prayer, taking up arms and hoes,
Tools of head and hand,
Purse and persuasion, hearts hardened to their foes,
With Jews' determination,
Calling it miracles.

Aunt Betty's Lemon Sauce

Once a year, the day
before Passover, I wash
out the double boiler,
stare at the curious pot,
never touched other
than on this occasion,
and prepare to prepare
Aunt Betty's lemon sauce.
Tangy, yellow, smooth,
a favorite family tradition,
no one would dare eat
the treat on any other day.

Heresy is to ladle it
on anything other
than sponge cake
made with potato starch
and matzo cake meal
dry as the Sinai
despite the six
large eggs added
to a simple syrup
of sugar and water.

Each year I think,
This is the year.
I will rebel, strike
out from family
and pick sweet
strawberries so juicy,
put them in a crystal
bowl and then cover
the fruit with the lemon
confection, perfection.

Yet, I cannot bring myself,
no matter how daring
I am grown up to be
to deviate from memory
of grandmother, mother
and long-gone Springs
and the traditions kept
that have given me wings.

True Legacy

My holiday table gleams,
Adorned with my Grandmothers'
China and candlesticks.
The scents of my Mother's
Recipes fill the house,
Welcoming family and friends.
Their pictures
Capturing moments in time,
Share spaces on my walls
And in my heart.
Yet their true legacy
Is in the intangibles.
In echoes of
The love they gave,
The examples they set,
The time they gave,
Their deeds of kindness.
I pray, that I too,
Am remembered that way.

Poem for Aaron

I want to honor your memory
Without the stab of pain
I want to remember you smiling
Sunshine—in pouring rain.

I want to remember the songs you wrote
The lyrics you worked to perfect
The instruments you took apart,
The moments when you could reflect.

I want to remember the joy I felt
The day that you were born
The love we felt in naming you
The family bond we formed.

I want to remember the boy you were
And the promise of a man
The jeans ripped and faded,
Baseball hat in hand.

The sports you loved to play
The trips we took each summer
The broken arm the first day at camp
The letters that started—and ended—
With "Dear Mother."

How you made us all laugh
And were a friend to all
How you trusted way too much
And grew to be so tall.

The way you accepted everyone
And wrote with your left hand
The birthmark on your tush
The trombone you played in band.

The way you were always "picked for everything"
The curiosity of your mind
The way you loved my baking
And how you were one-of-a-kind.

The way you "twiddled your pillow"
How handsome you looked in a tux
The way you loved Elyse
And were always "borrowing a buck."

The museum you set up in your room,
The shirts that smelled like you,
The way you reminded me of Dad,
The UGG slippers you considered shoes.

The way that we were four
And loved each other so
The way you hugged me all the time
And why you had to go.

Mom's Still Around . . . Watching and Guiding!

When I tune into my spirit-heart,
that's when advice from my late mother starts!

Now, she lovingly directs from the Heavens above . . .

Still coaching and prodding . . . they call that "tough love."

"I can see that you've not stuck to your diet, my dear."

(OY VEY... What did I do with that exercise gear??!!)

"You need to get moving and focus on health . . .

Remember, it's far more important than wealth!"

"You go out in the winter . . . I see you're half-dressed."

(But, I no longer wear sandals, so ya don't have to stress!)

"You wasted money in Vegas on gambling and shows . . ."

(Well . . . at least I didn't get arrested like someone we know!")

"I really like your hairstyle. Your gal *finally* got it right!"

(Wish you were here with your VISA card. That salon is out of sight!)

"I miss our late-night phone calls and our little sips of booze."

*(Now, I look up towards the heavenly skies
and tell you all my news.)*

"I'll continue to give sound advice—because
that's what Jewish mothers do.

And, I *know* that you'll be listening when I send my love to you."

Autumn Memories

I struggle each November remembering my parents' deaths years ago during that month. Each year I think that, if only I could believe in God, my grief and other difficult times might be tempered.

The sadness is triggered when I rake crunchy leaves, scratching open the old wounds. The sweeping motion, the familiar smell of dried leaves, the endeavor itself pulls me backward in time.

"You can push more leaves into that bag," my father would say, but only after he encouraged my sister and me to romp in them and to create a colorful haystack. "Never forget that wet leaves can be as slick as ice," my mother would caution, but only after she helped me track down the prettiest oranges and reds for my Brownie scrapbook.

Today I, a secular Jew, hear and feel my parents within my heart. I energetically rake and bag, but only after I build a gigantic mound of nature's cast-off palette. I help my husband discover the most gorgeous ones to mail to his daughter in dry Texas, and I am more careful than usual walking to temple on rainy days. I practice their life lessons, but still I crave to cushion their losses with a belief in God.

Now I realize that they, agnostics to the core, were teaching me to be industrious, to dance in the moment, to protect against danger, to recognize the truly beautiful.

"We don't believe in God," they would say, but nevertheless they lived their entire lives as though they did.

Grandma's Reply

You ask how I felt about not carrying Torah?
Ah, meydele, but I did carry Torah.
Not in my arms:
My arms were busy carrying children
And hiding children and burying children.
They were busy lighting candles
Which were cradled in the candlesticks
That I packed and carried and unpacked
And set on the table you knew so well.

Ah, meydele, but I did carry Torah.
I carried Torah in my heart and in my soul.
I carried it within me into the cellar,
And its words appeared on my lips in the boat.
I carried it within me as I packed and unpacked
    my candlesticks,
Those very same candlesticks your mother used
To help light your path toward Torah.

But, I pause now meydele,
For I know what I am telling you is true,
But it is only one truth among many.

How I yearned to touch and hold and hug our Torah,
How I yearned to be comforted in her embrace,
How saddened and confused I was
By the distance they created between us.
When I was frightened in that damp cellar,
I tried so hard to be comforted by the words of Torah,
But the only ones they let me learn were in the *V'ahavta*,
So I said them over and over and over,
As I rocked my children and waited for dawn.

And when I saw your mother running free and happy,
When I saw her black curls draped around
    her growing body,
I wanted so to touch and hold and hug our Torah,
I wanted so to express my joy and gratitude
    with words from the Torah,
But the only ones they let me learn were in the *V'ahavta,*
So I said them over and over and over,
Blessing and being blessed finding one form.

Ah, but how we women love being close up to
    what we cherish!
How we need to touch and feel and smell
    so that we know!
So go today and touch the Torah.
Feel in your hands the power and love
    that I know in my heart,
That my mother knew and that her mother knew.
And when you hug the Torah,
Hug it for me.
And when you read the Torah,
Say the words that I wanted to say, so long ago.
You know which they are.
From the depths of our hearts,
    we have passed them to you,
Now give them back to us with your voice.

Words We Did Not Share

I have no memories
of words
connecting
you to me.

On your ocean crossing
from "old country"
to "new,"
you *shlepped*
a carpetbag of language
that kept us apart.

No one ever thought
to feed the *mame-loschen*,
onto this grandchild's tongue.
But the flavored
words I heard
each Shabbos afternoon

bubbling
from the pot
of Yiddishkeit
you kept astir
with spoon in hand
wafted into me.

Nonetheless,
I did not envy
my neighbor friend,
whose Yiddish-speaking *bobbe*
lived in her family home.

I was grateful
that your house
was walking-blocks away

far enough
to keep me
from asking
what now I wish I knew—

if you stood
at your mother's elbow
as she kneaded
challah dough,

if you shyly
watched your father
as he *davened*
daily prayer,

if Simon came
to be your spouse,
by broker
or by choice.

The words
I never spoke,
when I hear
or read them,
or when
from nowhere
they pop
into my head,
summon you to me—

(continued)

four foot eight (or less),
baby soft inside my hug,
one eye closed forever
behind glasses rimmed in gold,
silver hair pulled back
and fastened in a knot—

so defined by age,
I could not imagine
you not being old

until now, as I write,
and imagine you
with hair
an autumn auburn,
the lovely color
I was told it was,
when you might
have worn it at your shoulders—
flowing and unbound.

SEEKING HEALING

In the Blink of an Eye

In the blink of an eye
The whole world changes
People that we love
Suddenly are gone
All that we have
Is but lent to us
In the blink of an eye
Ashes turn to dust

In the blink of an eye
Our lives flash before us
Thinking of things
That we should have done
Promises made, promises broken
In the blink of an eye
We feel so alone

We turn to the One
From whom we draw comfort
When family and friends
Aren't enough
We look for the strength
From deep inside us
The spirit of our loved one
Forever in our hearts

One Year Later—One Year a Widow

It is nearly a year,
Since your abrupt
Departure.
We will gather
Once again
At your gravesite
This time to see
Engraved in stone
The reality that
We have come
To accept
The reality that we
Do not want to accept.
Your family and
Your friends
Are here
Once again.
This saying "goodbye" thing
Takes time
And is so very
Hard.
Goodbye, my love
We miss you.
Rest in peace.

A Healing Prayer

Eternal God, Ruler of the Universe,
I pray for awareness and insight,
That my eyes might see
> In everything a mirror of the Divine Image.

That my eyes might see
> Beyond the concrete, the illusion, the apparent,
> Beyond simple good/bad and right/wrong
> to the paradox,
> Beyond the paradox to the underlying truth, and
> Beyond the truth to the Mystery
> that is known only to You.

That my eyes might see
> That You are farther than the stars
> But closer to me than my heart.

That my eyes might see
> Holiness and its spark present in all people,
> Including myself.

That my eyes might see
> All of Your gifts and blessings
> Even when they are in disguise.

That my eyes might see
> My oneness with my people
> And with all people who seek You in truth.

That my eyes might see
> A prayer answered,
> Even if it does not seem obvious,
> Or even desired.

That my eyes might see
> My true and holy role
> That You have promised and ordained,
> As no *less* than co-creator of this world.

Help me to accept this covenant
As my burden, my sacred duty,
my awesome responsibility,
And also my consummate privilege.
Help me also to understand
That I am no *more* than a co-creator
Of that which gives meaning to my life,
And that doing my part *is* enough.
That my eyes might see
The true Source of everything—
Of life and wisdom, of strength and peace,
Of worthiness and self-respect,
of wholeness and healing.
And also the source of my misery and pain,
Helplessness and hopelessness.
That my eyes might see
That real healing is not so much in the world
as in me,
And to understand at the deepest level of my being
That healing does not have to be sought
But is a gift already present,
And needs only to be recognized.
And help me to find
Rest, respite, restoration to wholeness
And to oneness with You and all people,
And healing for all the wounds of living.

I Will Make My Tears Holy

I will make my tears
Holy,
By living,
Living fully.
I will make my tears
Holy,
By giving more of me
To my grandchildren
To compensate for the loss of you.

I will make my tears
Holy,
By trying to live from
Your example.

I will make my tears
Holy,
By becoming involved in
Community and tzedakah.

I will make my tears
Holy,
By building new relationships
And having new experiences
And continuing to learn
And to grow, as you
Would have encouraged me.

I will make my tears
Holy,
By remaining connected
To your family, our family.

I will make my tears
Holy,
By remembering your love,
Your reassurance
And your belief in me.

I will make my tears
Holy,
By caring for others
Being a wise counsel,
And being the person
You believed I could be.

Becoming Thankful

Some days are just harder
A tug on an invisible string
I look fine, pretty good even
Always a sparkly smile
But what lies silent just below the surface?
At times it is hard to be thankful

It is easy to believe when life is good
How do I find you when I feel broken?
I return again to you, my God.

Hold me, Adonai
As I struggle with this pain.
I am willing to trust that there is a plan.
Thank you God.

Memories and Loss

Our hearts and minds do not follow the same rules.
One knows love; the other knows reason.
In conflict they fall, as our loved one's last breath is called.
The battle within persists.
It is easy to think it will never end.
Then one day clarity returns:
The mind no longer is a swirl;
The heart no longer aches unbearably;
The celebration of a life lost begins.
The tears of loss that marked the days
Turn into pleasant memories that once were shared.
The frowns of unending turmoil
Turn into soft smiles of happy times remembered.
The ache deep inside
Turns into the warmth and love of touching moments
    gone by,
Warmth that offers the comfort and peace of life
    celebrated, not lost
Embellished with thoughts of who we are because of all
    we shared.
Now our battle ends; our celebration lives within us.
Once again we can smile, laugh and live in peace.

As Life Continues

When you left our world years ago, I searched for you in everyone and everything. I clung to things you had loved as if to prove you once existed. I locked your memory away in my mind, not to share, but rather to rerun over and over again, not to forget the details.

As time has passed, many of your things have aged beyond repair or been lost in life's material jungle. And as for your memory, the details have faded, as if each year brought with it a translucent veil layered upon my looking glass.

Yet sorrow does not consume me, for now I know that all of your things, and the details of my memories, are not the keepsakes that gave your life value. Rather, they exist inside me—not in separate part, but in my wholeness.

The words I speak are framed by your perspective. The thoughts I think are founded in your wisdom. The actions I take mirror the ways you touched others beyond count.

My fingers can now release the grip of your things. My mind can quiet from the details of your life. For the evidence of your being is alive within me. I am myself, in part, because you lived.

CRJ 1972

Because I collected the quarters from the ashtray.
Because I removed the Betty Boop floor mats.
Because I placed the fishing rods from your trunk
    into my own.
Because I tossed the cushions, towels and that
    beaded seat cover.
Because I took two pairs of sunglasses and the auto wallet
    that smelled of Nautica.
Because I found the Nautica.
Because I kept the crate that contained baby wipes,
    upholstery cleaner, lighter fluid, flashlight,
    first-aid kit, silly umbrella hat and squeegee.
Because my hands assaulted your glove compartment,
    console and seat pockets.
Because I needed to touch everything your hands
    had touched.
Because I unearthed your emergency flare and
    medical supplies (all expired).
Because the Metallic Seattle Blue had only one dent
    after six months' use.
Because I sat where you sat against the grey velour
    upholstered seats.
Because it still had that new car scent you loved so.
Because I stood on line at the 34th Street DMV.
Because I clutched the plates to my chest and
    memorized them.
Because I had to sell your car.
Because I thought you would vanish from my thoughts.
Because then, and only then,
    I learned it doesn't work that way.

I Will Not Bury You

Our yard is full of the dead—
grey leaves, blanched stems,
bones dropped by raiding raccoons
on the dry winter grass.

The nearby graveyards are full,
their stones weathered, none
with crisp lines, no carefully-placed
pebbles to honor the dead.

There's nothing in our neighborhood.
What remains is too far off to visit
with the nightfall, so only the squirrels
will come to chatter about their days.

There's space in the graveyard near
our summer synagogue, a long way
from here, but not far from the beach
house. You can hear the sea.

There's room for us to join you once
we've raced our boats and built new castles.
For now we'll visit with the summer,
trailing sand from the beach. But after

we leave a whole year's stories
to weigh down your gravestone,
only the wind will be there
to hear you ask for just one more, so

I will not bury you.
I'll skip your gravestone pebbles
over the ocean, pour stories like sand,
wake you to hear.

Understanding the *Mi Shebeirach*

The fact that the new Lynne Landsberg cannot speak publicly with the ease of the old, is just one of a long list of deficiencies caused by my brain injury.

The *Mi Shebeirach*, which is a prayer for full recovery, recognizes different aspects of healing: *rifuat ha nefesh*, a healing of the *"nefesh"*—commonly translated as "soul," and *rifuat ha goof*, "healing of the body."

The healing of the body has come for me even more quickly than doctors had forecast. I am glad to report I have gone from a wheelchair and diapers to Ferragamo flats and Armani suits. However, my *rifuat ha nefesh* has been much slower. I think of *goof* as the outer self and *nefesh* as the thinking, feeling inner self—the all-encompassing "soul."

We know what it means to heal the body, but what does it mean to heal the soul? The healing of the *nefesh* requires one to accept certain harsh realities. My continued healing is dependent on my emotional ability to mourn the old Lynne Landsberg and to embrace the slowly developing skills of the new Lynne Landsberg.

I have learned to no longer measure my successes by comparing them to my former achievements. I now am thrilled and thank God every time I can do something new. Who ever thought that the ability to load the dishwasher was going to be divinely inspired?

Journaling/Praying

Journaling

Words pouring onto the paper
Relieving the heart
Smoothing out the emotions
Relief granted.

Praying

Words pouring into the heavens
Unburdening the heart
Channeling the feelings
May relief be granted.

A Prayer for Help

Dear God,

I'm not one who is accustomed to asking for help,
but I don't think I can handle this by myself any longer.
I, like other people (in this room), am hurting and
I do need Your help.

I have secrets I have never shared,
fears I've never admitted,
concerns I've never voiced . . . until now.

Give me the strength to live each day.
Grant me the courage to face my fears.
Remind me that I need not go through this alone.

Discover the Gifts

Eternal is Your power, O God; all life is a gift . . .

It is time
to discover the gifts
of dementia.
A disease we fear
like no other
striking what we believe makes us human.
We see only
the loss of self,
an empty shell.

It is a gift
to celebrate the quiet beauty
of the face creased by
a lifetime of blessings and sorrows.

The relationship that was
may be no more.
Yet, there is
never a complete loss of self,
never an empty shell!

A person remains
with capacity to love
and a spark of the Divine.

A new relationship awaits:
simply be present
cherish the repetition
the joy of singing
holding hands
brushing hair.

It is a gift
to set aside expectations
complicated histories
and just
be
with this person you love.

G'VUROT: GOD'S POWER

. . . With love You sustain the living,
With great compassion give life to all.
You send help to the falling and
Healing to the sick;
You bring freedom to the captive . . .

Give us Your strength,
Blessed One,
lift us
lovingly sustain us
free us.

Open our eyes
to this precious life.

Heal our hearts
as we receive this gift:
sacred moments,
to love and enjoy
our time together.

Blessed is the Eternal, the Source of life.

On Loss of a Partner

The body is there, the mind is not. One speaks, but receives no reply. I squeeze the hand, I kiss the lips I have known and loved for so many years. At best, there is a slight response; at worst, nothing.

What refuge is there from the loneliness of not being alone? I read aloud, though I know little is being absorbed. I play the music that he loves. We play games at which he was once expert, which he can now barely comprehend.

We go for a walk . . . my own walking now unsteady—the weak leading the weaker. Which is which?

We go for a drive amidst the beauties of nature—spring blossoms, summer's rich bounty. He barely looks.

What was once a duet is now a solo.

A friendly psychologist says "You are mourning a dead partnership." The diagnosis helps me understand my situation. Understanding brings some comfort.

So what can one do?

Of my friends of yore, the best are dead. I make new friends, some of them widows, like myself, others never married. I strengthen ties that were previously tenuous.

I listen to music.

I sit in my garden, where the varied shades of green soothe my eyes.

I meditate. Breathe in, breathe out. Let the calm enter and pervade the body. Let the inner eye wander back in recollection of a view, a setting that brought pleasure. Mountains, a lake, sea stretching to the horizon.

And amidst the loss, the solitude, the sadness— nevertheless the knowledge that the living body is still there, that I can embrace it and express my own love, my gratitude for the years of partnership, of mutual support, of like-mindedness, of shared pleasures and passions, of parenthood, of seeing children flourish, grandchildren mature, great-grandchildren coming into our world.

I thank You, Living Creator, compassionate God,
for preserving my soul.
Great is Your trust!

Glorious Day

It's a glorious day
full of sunshine
and hope
So they say.
I should venture outside
But I can't.
It is raining on my heart.

I should move forward
live my life.
Find those blessings
So they say.
But I can't.
It is raining on my heart.

How dare life go on?
Who let the sun
rise and set?
How could days go by?
When I can't.
So I say.
It is raining on my heart.

SHARING

OUR COVENANT

INVOCATIONS AND BENEDICTIONS

PRAYERS

INVOCATIONS AND BENEDICTIONS

A *Hineni* Prayer, As We Say Welcome

Hineni means "here I am." It appears in Torah in Genesis. Abraham speaks for all men and women when he replies to God by saying . . . "here I am." It is a spiritual as well as practical response to God, "to indicate his readiness." *Hineni* . . . I am ready, and I am here.

Hineni, we are all here tonight, each of us, because we choose to bring our unique gifts to this community. We are saying . . . I am ready, beloved God, to be my truest self, to be engaged in living by using my unique strength and talent, I am ready to use my mind and heart.

Hineni . . . I acknowledge God's wisdom which leads me to think, feel and love with integrity and joy.

Hineni . . . I stand with Eve, Sarah, Rachael, Rebecca, Leah, Esther, Dvorah, Naomi, Yoheved, Yael and Miriam. And may we take a moment to come into silence and to close our eyes and bring into our circle women we love or have loved, women of blessed memory, women who have been our mentors or friends.

Hineni . . . thank you for bringing us to this day and evening, *Shehecheyanu*.

Hineni . . . here I am, here we are.

Prayer to Open a Meeting

Dear God,
Know that I am growing, as are we all.
Keep me from becoming too talkative and, particularly,
keep me from falling into the tiresome habit
of expressing an opinion on every subject.
Release me from the craving to straighten out
everybody else's affairs.
Keep my mind free from the recital of endless details.
Give me wings to get to the point.
Give me grace to listen to others.
Help me be patient.
Teach me the glorious lesson that occasionally,
I might be mistaken.
Make me thoughtful—but not moody,
helpful but not pushy—
independent, yet able to accept another opinion
with diplomacy.
Free me of the notion that simply because I have lived
a long time, I am wiser.
If I do not approve of some of the changes in this
organization today, give me the understanding and
wherewithal to keep my silence.
Let us be mindful of all these things, O God,
so that we as WRJ/Sisterhood
[insert name of your organization]
can offer our best, in abundance.

The Future Is Ours

Honi and the Carob Tree: A Talmudic Tale

> One day, Honi the Circle Maker was walking on the road and saw a man planting a carob tree. Honi asked the man, "How long will it take for this tree to bear fruit?"
>
> The man replied, "Seventy years."
>
> Honi then asked the man, "And do you think you will live another seventy years and eat the fruit of this tree?"
>
> The man answered, "Perhaps not. However, when I was born into this world, I found many carob trees planted by my father and grandfather. Just as they planted trees for me, I am planting trees for my children and grandchildren so they will be able to eat the fruit of these trees."

We are so blessed to be a part of this Sisterhood.

Our foremothers built for us a community that has grown and prospered for so many years.

We have done them proud, continuing to grow, educate and inspire new generations.

Decisions are not always easy but they are always important.

We have gathered to further that process.

We ask you to be thoughtful and forward thinking as we deliberate on the future plans of this organization.

Adonai . . . we know You dwell wherever we let You in, wherever we seek You and whenever we need You.

Be with us now as we move into that future.

Opening Prayer

Let us give thanks for this opportunity
to come together in service ...

One day at a time
One challenge at a time
One blessing at a time

We cannot do it all at once.
But we can take one action
We can listen to one person
We can solve one problem
And always remember that despite any challenges,
    we have much good fortune and many blessings.

And when we take a fresh perspective,
Forget what we "know" and discover a new approach,
Sometimes we find that in tackling the challenge comes
a rare opportunity to reinvent ourselves
And in the reinvention, the perceived challenge disappears.

So as we come together to work for the future of
our movement and our sisterhoods,
Let's take it one day at a time
Solve one challenge at a time
Celebrate one blessing at a time
And, as one joins another, see what we can become.

Ken y'hi ratzon.

TIME WAS: An Invocation

TIME WAS is the PAST; those innocent days when we could lie on the grass, watch the clouds roll by, forming elephants, mountains, wondrous shapes in the cumulus nimbus. We could blow music through split blades of grass and find buttercups to hold under the chin. Our paper boats glided away on crystal waters to rivers and seas beyond our youthful horizon. When we dug holes in the sand, we knew China was at the other end, so we dug carefully, fearfully because the other end of the world was truly "the unknown."

Now, TIME IS, and the clouds carry acid rain, and the grass hides dangerous pesticides and the rivers and streams that were friendly and crystal clear carry dangers of which we never dreamed; and China is closer than we ever knew, and that is NOW!

But, TIME WILL BE is TOMORROW: Will we be able to make a difference? Will we be able to make a better, safer, cleaner world? Tomorrow is the FUTURE and it is ours if we make it so.

WHO ARE WE? We are daughters, sisters, mothers, granddaughters and grandmothers. We are women of faith, women of Reform Judaism. We draw our strength from the tradition, the Torah. But, we also draw strength from the fortitude, commitment and example of the courageous Jewish women who precede us.

Our lives have been etched in time by generations past,

(continued)

by the Jewish women who came across the ocean, to an unknown land, knowing neither language nor custom. With fortitude and faith they made a home, taught the Tradition, created a better future for themselves and for future generations of Jewish women.

Here, today, we follow their example. We come together to study, to pray, to share and to learn from each other; to reaffirm our faith in the past and our confidence in the future.

Because we link our minds and our spirits, we can face tomorrow, all the tomorrows that follow; renewed, refreshed, knowing that our past is done and our future is in each other's hands.

Invocation 1

God, our Creator and Teacher,

The One who embraces all of Creation
Bless those who have gathered here today.
Unite us in a holy singleness of purpose.
Encourage the work of our hands outstretched
    in Friendship.

May our tongues be innocent of malice
Our lips free of deceit.
May our eyes behold the beauty in one another
Our hearts be generous in Humility and Trust.
May we become partners in Peace.
As You have sustained us, may we sustain one another.

God of all ages, watch over our lives.
Imbue us with the Spirit to establish a kinder, gentler
    world in our time.
Guide us along a steady path so that we who serve one
    another may serve as Deliverers of Justice and Truth.

Invocation II

God of all Humanity,

At this quiet moment of reflection
We open our souls to You.

We have come together in praise of life's meaning,
grateful to gather in the spirit of Friendship
and Sharing.

As we awaken to the brightness of each new day,
may the strength of our purpose be truly heightened.

Continue to bless us with Courage, Insight,
Patience and Endurance to preserve that which has been
entrusted to us.

May a sweeter softness return to our often harsh
and unkind world.

Your greatest gift to us is Life.

May our lives know greater meaning as we strive to make
a better world for all.

Empower us to do deeds of Merit as we foster Love over
hatred, Respect over prejudice, Peace over discord.

May we be worthy of our many Blessings and
share with one another our abundance in Peace.

Invocation III

God of all Nations,

We gather today with a kindred spirit
Committed to strengthening ties between one another,
With a genuine concern for all peoples regardless of
Race or creed.

May we be reminded to give freely of ourselves
To hearken to our voice of Conscience
That guides us to spiritually embrace our brethren
In an effort to break down those walls that
Ultimately can divide us.

Through sharing commonalities and respecting differences,
May we model for those whose hearts are
Tainted with bias
And follow a path of richness
Gained by fostering a world free of
Prejudice and Discrimination.

May we be inspired to interact as partners in Peace
Imbued with the fortitude to perpetuate a kinder,
More caring world.

May we strive to elevate our hearts and souls
As we awaken to the beauty of each new day
And reflect upon our many Blessings
To be shared with one another
In the pursuit of Holiness, Truth,
Justice and Peace.

Invocation IV

God of all Generations,

You who have always been our hope
Our Rock in times of trial and anguish,
Bless those who gather here today.

Guide us each day as we partner with one another
To preserve the gifts of Freedom, Community,
Justice and Peace.

May our eyes behold each other's beauty
May our hands reach outward in Friendship and Trust
May we foster that wondrous spirit of Brotherhood
In an effort to make our world a better place.

May Tolerance and Understanding
Shelter us from life's storms
Diffusing the turmoil that tends to surround us.

May we find contentment in giving and in giving
May we find hope.

As we are about to share our meal, may we contemplate
Our many blessings, and remain committed to
Making a difference
Elevating our souls,
Enriching not only our lives
But the lives of others.

Community Invocation for Ecumenical Dinner

Dear Lord . . . we give thanks unto You this day, for uniting the members of this interfaith community, in friendship. Though we worship You in different ways, we come together in the understanding that You are indeed of a divine nature. Together we feel Your loving kindness through our many blessings, especially the ability to walk hand-in-hand on the righteous path You've provided us. With each step we ask that our differences decrease so that we are better able to revel in our similarities while taking on the work we have been called upon to accomplish.

At this time, we ask for Your guidance in our quest to repair the world. May You, the G-d of Mercy, use us to accomplish the tasks needed to comfort all who suffer. Continue to give us strength and wisdom on this journey towards our goals. May our deeds shine as an example of what neighbors are able to achieve through good will and respect. In a Franciscan Monastery it was once said:

> May G-d bless us with enough foolishness to believe
> that we really can make a difference in this world, so
> that we are able, with G-d's grace, to do what others
> claim cannot be done.

May it please our respective deities, whether it is the G-d of Abraham or Jesus, that this interfaith alliance continues to co-exist for the greater good of others. Let the teachings within the Torah and the compassionate words of the Beatitudes always be at the heart of our endeavors.

(continued)

Rabbi Harold Kushner writes:

Let the rain come and wash away the ancient grudges,
the bitter hatreds held and nurtured over
generations.

Let the rain wash away the memory of the hurt,
the neglect.

Then let the sun come out and fill the sky with
rainbows.

Let the warmth of the sun heal us wherever we are
broken.

Let it burn away the fog so that we can see each other
clearly.
So that we can see see beyond
labels, beyond accents, gender or skin color.

Let the warmth and the brightness of the sun
melt our selfishness.
So that we can share the
joys and feel the sorrows of our neighbors.

And let the light of the sun be so strong that we
will see all people as our neighbors.

Let the earth, nourished by the rain, bring forth
flowers to surround us with beauty.

And let the mountains teach our hearts to reach
upward to heaven.

Amen

Closing Prayer

As our meeting closes, it seems that we are ending,
But we are really
Beginning
In challenging and changing times
Yet exciting times,
There is opportunity.
We can face it and make the most of it
Or we can just let whatever happens, happen

But . . . we are not women who "let it happen . . ."
No, **WE** *make* it happen

That you are here today says that you are
A woman of conscience and action
You will not only sustain our world,
You want to rejuvenate it—physically and spiritually
As do I

As did the women who came before us
                    As they expect us to do together
                                        As we shall . . .

And so we begin . . . *plus forte ensemble*—stronger together. . .

PRAYERS

Touch Me, God

Touch me, God.
>Help me find the path to know Your will.
>Inside, my feelings stir elusively.
>Joy, love, fear, regret—the list is long.

Touch me, God.
>I'm not afraid to know the place in me
>Where those emotions dwell.
>Yet, it is as if an inner spark still struggles to ignite.

Touch me, God.
>Open my eyes to see Your presence.
>I pray to recognize Your place within my being.
>Calm this din so deep inside.

Touch me, God.
>Release the hidden lock that bars my way.
>Let me journey to the place of understanding.
>Shine Your light upon my heart—my soul.

Alas, a place within me—that center of my being—
seems afire
>With a yearning for Your touch.
>Could this be the place
>Where You have already touched me?

Wait, God, please!

I want to touch You back.

Open Up My Heart

Open up my heart
And fill it full of blessing
Open up my spirit
So I may listen well
To the voice,
The still, small voice
Within.
Crumble away the fear
And forgive the transgressions
Done in pain and anger
Redeemed through patience
Understanding
Awareness
And love.

Praise God

Praise God for the breath of life
    Praise God for the gift of song
Praise God for the open eye
    Praise God for the world to see
Praise God for the beating heart
    Praise God for the heart to love
Praise God for the hands to hold
    Praise God for the hands to give
Praise God for the feet to dance
    Praise God for the path to walk

Praise God for the words to praise
    Hallelujah, hallelujah.

Thank You God

Thank You God
for being there
when I needed You most.
There were moments
during this process
when I didn't know
if I would survive
or not.

But You knew
that I would
and You made that
possible.
You protected me
under Your wings,
You held me close,
You gave me strength,
courage,
and faith.
I am here today
because of You
and for that
I am most grateful.

Avodah—In the Quiet Time of Worship

In the quiet time of worship
We call you, Adonai
Please listen and grant our heart's request,
To be with us through our day, to protect the ones
      we love,
And to help us remember that You are never too far—
Just a thought, a word, a prayer away from all of us,
      Your Chosen

Oh, Compassionate One of Israel,
Accept the sincerity with which we pray for ourselves,
      for our people, for our world
May our Consciousness of You
Embrace each action that we take
And allow us to recall the nearness of Your Presence
Created in this quiet time of worship

For a Woman Diagnosed with Breast Cancer

Eloheinu v'Elohei Imoteinu. Our God and God of our Mothers. God of Sarah, Rebecca, Rachel, Leah, Miriam, Deborah, and Ruth: bless [*name*] as You have blessed our ancestors for generations. Give [*name*] the strength to get through this difficult time. Keep her from despair and guide her lovingly to a life of blessings. Grant her Sarah's ability to laugh, Miriam's direct connection to You, and Deborah's courage to fight this battle. Envelop [*name*] with the warmth of family, friends, and the many strangers rooting for her recovery.

Our God and God of our Mothers, draw us close to you. Resolve the discords of our lives. Renew our hopes and heal us, body and soul. *Adonai, atah rofei hacholim.* God of healing, listen as I speak the words Moses spoke to You years ago in the desert. *Eil na r'fa na lah.* Please God, bring healing and comfort to her. Bring healing to [*name*] as you brought healing to Miriam, the prophetess and beloved sister of Moses. Bring peace and comfort to [*name*] and her family, *Adonai.* Bring peace. *Oseh shalom bimromav, hu yaaseh shalom aleinu v'al kol Yisrael.*

A Prayer before Breast Cancer Treatment

In the Torah You are called El Shaddai, as a warrior.
Then You fought the Egyptians,
Now I need You to fight for me.

This is not typically how I turn to You,
But circumstances are different.
And I'm different too.

I call upon You now, El Shaddai,
God of my breasts.
Give me the courage to face each day's treatment.
Help me to stay as calm and as present as I can be.
Give me the strength to endure any pain or any shame.
Bless my doctors with wisdom and their hands
    with gentleness.
May their lips speak words of compassion
    in ways I'll understand
And may I know to ask another simply to hold my hand.

Hazak, Hazak v'Nithazek
You'll be strong, and I'll be strong, and let us emerge
    even stronger.
Blessed are You, El Shaddai, God of my breasts,
    my personal warrior.

Hashkiveinu

Hashkiveinu Adonai . . .

Watch over us while we sleep, keep us safe.
Keep us safe from bad dreams coming true.

> *Keep our children safe from bullies and from others*
> *who would hurt them.*

Keep our parents safe from harsh realities of growing old,
from the sense of loneliness and loss.

> *Keep our friends safe from losing their jobs and their*
> *homes while they struggle to stay afloat.*

And keep those on the street safe from the cold, sickness
and hunger.

> *Keep the child safe who has no parent to protect her,*
> *no one to tell her who she is.*

Keep those safe with mental illness or any kind of illness and
who are challenged to deal with every day life stresses.

> *Keep safe our soldiers who commit themselves to*
> *our country.*

And keep our police and firefighters safe who are there to
protect us.

> *Keep our teachers safe who are truly on the front lines.*

Keep the stranger safe for he may be our friend in
another time.

*Keep our community safe for it is the infrastructure
of tomorrow.*

Keep our clergy safe so they may comfort and guide us.

*And keep Israel safe for it is our past, our present and
our future.*

And when we awake, may we know how we've been blessed.

Springtime

We thank you God
- for the wondrous world in which we live
- for the food that nourishes our bodies
- for the beauty that only you can create
  with the freshness and new growth of spring
- for acquaintances who have become our friends
- for the strangers who have become our
  acquaintances and
- for the ability to learn and grow from
  everything we do.

May we who enjoy abundance never forget those
who are less fortunate.

God, watch over all of us and bless us with peace
and harmony.

A Prayer for New Members

May the One who blessed our ancestors, bless all of those who have come forward tonight to become a part of our community.

We give thanks that the varied paths of their lives have led them here, and that we will have the blessing of accompanying them on these next steps of their journey.

May they be blessed here with opportunities for the sacred work that sustains our lives and the world we live in, in the realms of *Torah, Avodah,* and *G'milut Chasadim*—study, prayer, and acts of loving kindness. May this synagogue be to them a place to preserve ancient traditions and create new ones, a place to learn and grow, a place to be challenged, strengthened and spiritually uplifted.

Like Abraham and Sarah, whose tent was open on all sides to welcome the stranger, may we open our tents and our arms wide in welcome, so that all may come to feel at home in this congregation.

Help us to move from swimming in a sea of strangers to finding many familiar and friendly faces. Help us soon to reach that moment where our friends become our family.

May we know the blessing of learning, praying, and pursuing justice together, sharing the joy of our simchas, supporting each other in times of difficulty, and comforting one another in times of sorrow. So may all of us take part in building a *mishkan,* a holy dwelling place, and a *k'hilah k'dushah,* a sacred community.

A Prayer for Marriage Equality

God who is Parent, Partner, and Friend, we thank You for the gift of Your love. Your love inspired You to create us in Your image. Your love knows no boundaries of religion or race, sexuality or gender. We give thanks for the ability to love one another, and to create families through our love. We give thanks for the ability to fight intolerance with our love, and for Your commandment to love our neighbors as ourselves.

We ask for Your guidance as we fight to protect those we love. Grant wisdom to our community's leaders and citizens. Give us the courage to speak up for the rights of the disenfranchised. Give us patience in the face of intolerance.

Guide us as we strive to fulfill the prophecy of Jeremiah (33:10–1): "Soon may there be heard, throughout the cities of Judah and the streets of Jerusalem, the voice of happiness and the voice of jubilation, the voice of the bridegroom and the voice of the bride."

May these voices never be silenced: the voices of bride and groom, of bride and bride, of groom and groom, of parents and their children. We pray that the day may come soon when all shall know the joy of love that can be celebrated under the canopy and in the courthouse, supported by family and community, and upheld and sustained by law.

Blessed are You God, Source of Love,
Creator and Protector of Families.

A Prayer for Mothers with Handicapped Children

I watch my son, confident and tall
Standing on the bimah
Sharing memories of his Jewish experiences
Praying at the Western Wall
Climbing Masada at dawn
Standing under the chuppah
Naming his daughter
The bris for the son
And my heart fills with joy, the Jewish mother's dream
L' dor vador
But there is the other son
The son whose words are locked in silence
The son who will not marry
Who will have no children to carry on his name
With a sense of sadness, I ask why
But we are not alone, we mothers of the "different" child
Although the differences are many, the sadness is the same
The sadness of lost hopes, lost joy, and guilt
And always asking why
But faith in Judaism gives us a foundation
And Sisterhood gives us a "family"
To look beyond lost opportunities
To find new ways to look at the world
Our faith in Judaism provides solace, comfort, and support
Adonai, please bless us and give us the courage and
strength to meet life's challenges and to always find
comfort in the arms of our sisters

A Caregiver's Blessing

May the One who blessed our ancestors, bless those in
our community who care for others. Grant them strength
and patience, a gentle hand and a listening ear, as they
perform the *mitzvah* of caring for those who are ill.
Be to them a Rock in the difficult moments of their daily
routine; a Refuge in times of crisis. Give them the
courage to seek help when they need it, and give us the
wisdom and compassion to be responsive to their needs
and the needs of their families. When healing is possible,
may their loved ones be healed and strengthened.
When illness lingers, grant peace to those who are
suffering and those who are watching their loved ones
suffer. May their care be received with gratitude and love.

A Prayer for Peace

Poems have been written, songs have been sung
A prayer on the lips of the old and the young
Hearts have yearned for peace to be
The sacred place of community
Still, in towns and cities, nations worldwide
Fathers have mourned, mothers have cried
To see precious children go to war
All the flowers have gone, to return home no more

What will it take, we asked of each other,
To build lasting peace, to love one another
To put down our weapons and push egos aside
To go toward the light where Shechinah resides
To have respect and compassion, embrace others for being
All creatures of earth, with hurts worthy of healing?
The intent, is our answer, peace in action and word
Sim Shalom, Adonai, let our voices be heard!

CLOSING POEM

My Wish for You, My Daughter

May your days be filled with light from within.

May you always remember
that you are made in God's image.

May you be gentle with yourself.

May you love others with the fullness of your heart.

May you find passion in your pursuits.

May God find favor in all your deeds.

May others speak of you with honor.

May you leave this world
knowing that you have been a blessing to others.

ACKNOWLEDGMENTS

Covenant of the Generations could not have been published without the participation of many dedicated individuals, whose work we gratefully acknowledge:

The creative and talented writers who shared their gifts for us all to enjoy.

The WRJ Covenant Book Committee:
 Sherri Feuer, Chair
 Betty Weiner, Co-Chair
 Rabbi Marla J. Feldman, WRJ Executive Director
 Lynn Magid Lazar, WRJ President
 Blair Marks, WRJ First Vice President
 Rosanne Selfon, Centennial Chair
 Diane Kaplan, Centennial Co-Chair
 Sara Charney, WRJ Vice President
 Susan Pittelman, WRJ Board Member

Selection Review Team:
 Sara Charney   Roberta Krolick
 Rabbi Joan Glazer Farber   Lynn Magid Lazar
 Rabbi Marla J. Feldman   Blair Marks
 Sherri Feuer   Susan Pittelman
 Lois Gibson   Rosanne Selfon
 Diane Kaplan   Betty Weiner

The copy editors, who painstakingly reviewed this publication:
 Susan Pittelman, Senior Editor
 Susan Bass
 Amanda Feldman
 Sherri Feuer
 Betty Weiner

(continued)

The WRJ staff members, who facilitated the process of creating this publication:
 Amanda Feldman, Manager of Meetings and Programs
 Carolyn Kunin, Director of Programs and Advocacy (retired)
 Toba Strauss, WRJ Intern from the Hebrew Union College-
 Jewish Institute of Religion

WRJ President Lynn Magid Lazar, First Vice President Blair Marks, and Executive Director Rabbi Marla J. Feldman, whose support, encouragement, and enthusiasm were invaluable in bringing this book to print.

Rabbi Rachel Hertzman, for writing the beautiful opening prayer.

David Sandman and Jeff Goffman of The Goffman Group, for shepherding this publication through the design and printing process.

Our generous donors, without whom *Covenant of the Generations* would not have been possible:
 Congregation Schaarai Zedek Sisterhood, Tampa, Florida
 Lynn Magid Lazar and Dale S. Lazar
 Norma U. Levitt, through the Norma U. Levitt Publication Fund
 of Women of Reform Judaism

CONTRIBUTORS

Sisterhood: A Covenant of the Generations

Based on Exodus 38:8: "He [Bezalel] made the laver of copper and its stand of copper, from the mirrors of the women who performed tasks at the entrance of the Tent of Meeting."
Rabbi Rachel Hertzman
Temple Ner Tamid, Montclair, New Jersey

LIVING OUR COVENANT | Sisterhood

The Twenty-First Century Jewish Woman
Peggy (Ryfkah) Horwitz
Temple Beth Ohr, La Mirada, California

My Sisters
Laurel Burch Fisher
Temple Shalom, Dallas, Texas

Being Part of a Sacred Community
This poem was developed with the Sisterhood women from San Antonio, Texas.
Rosanne Selfon
Congregation Shaarai Shomayim, Lancaster, Pennsylvania

This Is Sisterhood
Naida Cohn
Stephen Wise Free Synagogue, New York, New York

Of Sisters
Edith Caplan
Temple Beth Torah, Fremont, California

Sisters by Choice
Myra Feiger
Temple Sinai, Oakland, California

The Light of God
Trina Novak
Temple Beth Shalom, Needham, Massachusetts

Fertile Ground
Denise Fogel
Temple Israel, Minneapolis, Minnesota

Sarah's Tent
Amy Willis
Temple Beth Shalom, Needham, Massachusetts

Our Divine Spark
Denise Fogel
Temple Israel, Minneapolis, Minnesota

LIVING OUR COVENANT | Women of Reform Judaism

A Sanctuary for Our Jewish Lives
These words were inspired, in part, by the writings of Dolores K. Wilkenfeld.
Naida Cohn
Stephen Wise Free Synagogue, New York, New York

The Feeling of Sisterhood
Ilene Lanin-Kettering
Beth Tikvah Congregation, Hoffman Estates, Illinois

Pursuing Justice
Cynthia Roosth Wolf
Temple Emanuel, Beaumont, Texas

A Tree of Life
Elaine Shapiro
Shir Ami, Newtown, Pennsylvania

On Becoming a Leader
Denise Fogel
Temple Israel, Minneapolis, Minnesota

CELEBRATING OUR COVENANT | Shabbat

Preparing for Shabbat
Esther M. Nathanson
Temple Sinai, Pittsburgh, Pennsylvania

Become One
Laurel Burch Fisher
Temple Shalom, Dallas, Texas

Turning Point
Ariel Lee
Temple Shalom, Winnipeg, Manitoba, Canada

Shabbat Prayer
Karen Tanner
Temple Sinai, Oakland, California

Gather in Shabbat
Angela Banker
Temple Emanu-El, Dothan, Alabama

Shabbat
Maryann Fenster
University Synagogue, Los Angeles, California

Zachor
Rena Riback Geffen
Central Synagogue of Nassau County, Rockville Centre, New York

Shabbos
Maxine Boshes
Congregation B'nai Israel, Sacramento, California

For Shabbat
Nancy Lee Gossels
Temple Shir Tikva, Wayland, Massachusetts

Kol Isha Prayer for Candle Lighting
This prayer may be said when lighting Shabbat candles or at a service honouring women.
Ariel Lee
Temple Shalom, Winnipeg, Manitoba, Canada

CELEBRATING OUR COVENANT | Holidays

Washing Windows in Elul
Carolyn Litwin
Temple Beth Sholom, Topeka, Kansas

The Sound of Shofar
Nancy Lee Gossels
Temple Shir Tikva, Wayland, Massachusetts

Here I Am, God
Nancy Lee Gossels
Temple Shir Tikva, Wayland, Massachusetts

Kol Nidrei
Sara Luria
Hebrew Union College-Jewish Institute of Religion, New York, New York

Yom Kippur
Sophia Twersky, age 15
Temple Beth Am, Seattle, Washington

Sonnet on the Book of Life
© 2005 by Lynn Levin
Originally published in *Poetica Magazine* (Summer 2005):15; also appeared in *Poetica Magazine: Yom Kippur Edition* (Fall 2011):12. Reprinted by permission of the author.
Lynn Levin
Southampton, Pennsylvania

Pesach *Yizkor*
Rabbi Jennifer Gubitz
Temple Shir Tikva, Wayland, Massachusetts

Strangers on the Seder Plate
Carolyn Litwin
Temple Beth Sholom, Topeka, Kansas

The Four WRJ Daughters
Marlen D. Frost
Temple Israel, Omaha, Nebraska

The Journey Never Ends
Nancy Lee Gossels
Temple Shir Tikva, Wayland, Massachusetts

This Is Our Story Too
Rabbi Leah Doberne-Schor
Tree of Life Congregation, Columbia, South Carolina

Fasting on *Tisha B'Av*, 5757
Eve Lyons
Brighton, Massachusetts

HONORING OUR COVENANT | The Shoah

The Nut Brown Sweater
Julie Standig
The Community Synagogue, Port Washington, New York

Collections at Auschwitz
Ahuva Zaches
Hebrew Union College-Jewish Institute of Religion, Los Angeles, California

Warsaw Ghetto, November 2008
Julie Standig
The Community Synagogue, Port Washington, New York

Man Does Not Live by Bread Alone
Based on Parashat Eikev
Sarah B. Schweitz
Temple Beth Sholom of Orange County, Santa Ana, California

HONORING OUR COVENANT | Israel

A Prayer for Israel
Linda P. Zoll
Congregation Emanu El, Houston, Texas

Open a Gate for Us at the Closing of a Gate: A Prayer for Days of Political
Disagreement in Israel
*The title was based on the liturgy of the High Holy Days. The last stanza was based on
Psalms 51:12.*
Translated from the original Hebrew by Rabbi David Nelson.
Rabbi Dr. Dalia Marx
Hebrew Union College-Jewish Institute of Religion, Jerusalem, Israel

Standing at the Wall: An *Ahavah Rabbah* Prayer
© 2011 by Rabbi Miriam Philips
With thanks to Debbie Friedman
Rabbi Miriam Philips
Temple Emanuel, Andover, Massachusetts

At the Wall
Sophia Twersky, age 15
Temple Beth Am, Seattle, Washington

Jerusalem
(1980s)
Previously published in *Hearing Beyond Sound* by Elaine M. Starkman. San Ramon, CA:
dvs publishing, 2012. Reprinted by permission of the author.
Elaine M. Starkman
Walnut Creek, California

My Jerusalem
Marla Goldberg
Temple Beth Israel, Skokie, Illinois

EMBRACING OUR COVENANT | Life Cycles

God-like
Excerpt from *Because Nothing Looks Like God* © 2001 by Lawrence and Karen
Kushner. Reprinted by permission of the authors.
Sara Luria
Hebrew Union College-Jewish Institute of Religion, New York, New York

Prayer for the Birth of a Child
Phyllis Bigelson
Temple Ahavat Shalom, Northridge, California

Prayers for Mothers Giving Birth
Rabbi Corrie Zeidler
Ma'alot Tivon Congregation, Tivon, Israel

Growing a Grandmother's Heart
*My teachers, Rabbi Harold Schulweis and Reb Zalman Shacter-Shalomi, have grandmother
hearts. To them and to my grandmothers, I dedicate these words.*
Rabbi Malka Drucker
Santa Fe, New Mexico

Daughter of the Covenant: A Bat Mitzvah Meditation
Ariel Lee
Temple Shalom, Winnipeg, Manitoba, Canada

Bar Mitzvah
(January 2006)
Suzanne Gallant
Temple Adat Elohim, Thousand Oaks, California

Prayer for Our Graduating Seniors
Cantor Pamela Siskin
Congregation Beth Israel, West Hartford, Connecticut

A Blessing for Students Going to Israel
Rabbi Leah Berkowitz
Judea Reform Congregation, Durham, North Carolina

There Are No Size 12 Shoes in the Hallway
Abigail Fisher
Beth El Temple Center, Belmont, Massachusetts

Singing the *Sh'ma* for My Dad
Jeanette Gross
Temple Isaiah, Lafayette, California

How Have I Lived?
Linda P. Zoll
Congregation Emanu El, Houston, Texas

REFLECTING ON OUR COVENANT | Living Jewishly

A Psalm to Friendship: An Acrostic
Diane Kaplan
Temple Israel, Minneapolis, Minnesota

Forever Friends
Originally published in *Feeling My Way – 99 Poetic Journeys* by Minx Boren. Palm Beach
Gardens, FL: Coach Minx Inc., 2008. Reprinted by permission of the author.
Minx Boren
Congregation B'nai Israel, Boca Raton, Florida

Sisterhood in a Splash: Standing at the Edge of the Mikveh
Claudia Teitelbaum
Congregation Beth Israel, West Hartford, Connecticut

My Mikveh Experience
Resa Davids
University Synagogue, Los Angeles, California

She Leaves Nothing to Chance
Melissa Faber
Temple Israel, Memphis, Tennessee

Convert: A New Story
*This poem came out of a women's writing class assignment; we were asked to share
memories of Kabbalat Shabbat with our mothers or grandmothers. I wrote this for women
who come to Judaism as adults, and have to create their own traditions.*
Sara Ben-Ami
Temple Beth El, Madison, Wisconsin

Must a Jewish Mother Be Jewish?
Patti Freeman Dorson
Indianapolis Hebrew Congregation, Indianapolis, Indiana

Have Patience, Dear Sister
Cynthia Roosth Wolf
Temple Emanuel, Beaumont, Texas

What Might You Be Willing

Originally published in *Feeling My Way – 99 Poetic Journeys* by Minx Boren. Palm Beach Gardens, FL: Coach Minx Inc., 2008. Reprinted by permission of the author.
Minx Boren
Congregation B'nai Israel, Boca Raton, Florida

Soaking in Torah

Rabbi Jennifer Gubitz
Temple Shir Tikva, Wayland, Massachusetts

Thank You, *Shechinah*

Susan Pittelman
Congregation Shalom, Milwaukee, Wisconsin

A Jewish Legacy

(Passover, 14 Nissan 5766)
Denise Sherer Jacobson
Temple Sinai, Oakland, California

To Life

Pia Taavila
Beth Sholom Temple, Fredericksburg, Virginia

Arvit (Evening Prayer)

Tsipi Keller
West Palm Beach, Florida

Just Be Nice

Beverly J. Smith
Temple B'nai Israel, Albany, Georgia

Jewish Girl's Guide to Guacamole

Originally published in *Poetica Magazine* (November 2006): 19. Reprinted by permission of the author.
Ellen Sazzman
Temple Sinai, Washington, DC

We Are None of Us Wise Enough Alone

© by Minx Boren
Minx Boren
Congregation B'nai Israel, Boca Raton, Florida

REFLECTING ON OUR COVENANT | Talking to God

Noah's Wife Talks Back
Eve Lyons
Brighton, Massachusetts

Creation Prayer
Judith Luck Sher
Temple Israel, Minneapolis, Minnesota

Mi Chamochah
Ahuva Zaches
Hebrew Union College-Jewish Institute of Religion, Los Angeles, California

Thought for the Day
Julie Galambush
Temple Micah, Washington, DC

Small Voices
Rena Riback Geffen
Central Synagogue of Nassau County, Rockville Centre, New York

Be a *Sukka* to Me (*or* A Jewish Matryoshka)
Translated from the original Hebrew by Jessica Sacks.
Rabbi Dr. Dalia Marx
Hebrew Union College-Jewish Institute of Religion, Jerusalem, Israel

A Reflection on Holiness
Rabbi Alison Abrams
Temple Chai, Long Grove, Illinois

Zusha at Lake Tahoe
Previously published in *Hearing Beyond Sound* by Elaine M. Starkman. San Ramon, CA: dvs publishing, 2012. Reprinted by permission of the author.
Elaine M. Starkman
Walnut Creek, California

Listen, My Soul, Listen
Ariel Lee
Temple Shalom, Winnipeg, Manitoba, Canada

Asher Yatzar
Ahuva Zaches
Hebrew Union College-Jewish Institute of Religion, Los Angeles, California

How Can I Ask?
Originally published in *Yoga Shalom* by Lisa Levine with Carol Krucoff. New York:
URJ Press, 2011. Reprinted by permission of the URJ Press.
Cantor Lisa Levine
Temple Shalom, Chevy Chase, Maryland

Oneness
Originally published in *Yoga Shalom* by Lisa Levine with Carol Krucoff. New York:
URJ Press, 2011. Reprinted by permission of the URJ Press.
Cantor Lisa Levine
Temple Shalom, Chevy Chase, Maryland

A Meditation on *Ma'ariv Aravim*
For Rabbi Fred Reiner
Judy Neri
Temple Sinai, Washington, DC

I Wonder With Wonder
Deborah Ross
Temple Shalom, Aberdeen, New Jersey

DRAWING STRENGTH FROM OUR COVENANT | Legacies

Sh'ma
Kate Royston
Congregation Beth Israel, Portland, Oregon

Avot v'Imahot, A Prayer of My Legacy
Denise Sherer Jacobson
Temple Sinai, Oakland, California

On Giving Thanks
Ravelle Brickman
Central Synagogue, New York, New York

The Flow of Generations
Norma U. Levitt
Temple Beth-El, Great Neck, New York

Pardes: My Neighbor's Garden
Sharon Singer Salinger
Temple Beth Shalom, Needham, Massachusetts

Torah Romance
Ellen Sazzman
Temple Sinai, Washington, DC

Reasons and Voices
Drema Yates
Temple Emanuel, Roanoke, Virginia

Peaches, Netanya, 1970
Previously published in *Hearing Beyond Sound* by Elaine M. Starkman. San Ramon, CA:
dvs publishing, 2012. Reprinted by permission of the author.
Elaine M. Starkman
Walnut Creek, California

Two Crones
Originally published in *Soul Notes* by Minx Boren. Palm Beach Gardens, FL:
Fourfold Path, 2000. Reprinted by permission of the author.
Minx Boren
Congregation B'nai Israel, Boca Raton, Florida

The Number Three
Hilda Glazer
Temple Beth Shalom, New Albany, Ohio

Low Country Jewess Comes of Age and Confronts History
Caren B. Masem
Temple Emanuel, Greensboro, North Carolina

Ode to Chicken Soup
Lois Gibson
Temple Israel, Minneapolis, Minnesota

Shalom Haverah (Friend)
Dedicated to Risa Sue Olmezer, of blessed memory (1942–1963)
Carol J. Wechsler Blatter
Temple Emanu-El, Tucson, Arizona

Ancestral Voices
Linda Hepner
Los Angeles, California

Aunt Betty's Lemon Sauce
Caren B. Masem
Temple Emanuel, Greensboro, North Carolina

True Legacy
Trina Novak
Temple Beth Shalom, Needham, Massachusetts

Poem for Aaron
In memory of Aaron Feuer z'l (1987–2008)
Sherri Feuer
Temple Israel, Minneapolis, Minnesota

Mom's Still Around ... Watching and Guiding!
Emily Audra Fleisher
Temple Beth Shalom, Hudson, Ohio

Autumn Memories
(December 1, 2011)
Diane K. Rudov
Temple Sinai, Pittsburgh, Pennsylvania

Grandma's Reply
Originally published in "So Go Today and Touch the Torah: A Family Story," *Journal of Feminist Family Therapy* 9, no. 4 (1997): 43-48. Reprinted by permission of Routledge: Taylor & Francis Group.

To Grandma Sadie, who arrived from Kladowa, Poland, in 1920, with her husband and two of her three children after surviving too many pogroms. Her eldest son, Motl, did not get permission to leave, and she never saw him again. None of her extended family survived the Holocaust. This poem was written thirty years after Grandma Sadie's death for the occasion of my adult Bat Mitzvah.
Marsha Mirkin
Auburndale, Massachusetts

Words We Did Not Share
For Julia (Yahla) Sandstein Abrams (1879 – 1953)
Carolyn Litwin
Temple Beth Sholom, Topeka, Kansas

DRAWING STRENGTH FROM OUR COVENANT |
Seeking Healing

In the Blink of an Eye
Originally published in *Yoga Shalom* by Lisa Levine with Carol Krucoff. New York: URJ Press, 2011. Reprinted by permission of the URJ Press.
Cantor Lisa Levine
Temple Shalom, Chevy Chase, Maryland

One Year Later—One Year a Widow
Suzanne Gallant
Temple Adat Elohim, Thousand Oaks, California

A Healing Prayer
Myrna Williamson
Temple Beth El, Madison, Wisconsin

I Will Make My Tears Holy
Suzanne Gallant
Temple Adat Elohim, Thousand Oaks, California

Becoming Thankful
Laurel Burch Fisher
Temple Shalom, Dallas, Texas

Memories and Loss
Angela Banker
Temple Emanu-El, Dothan, Alabama

As Life Continues
Katie Roeper
Congregation Beth Ahabah, Richmond, Virginia

CRJ 1972
Julie Standig
The Community Synagogue, Port Washington, New York

I Will Not Bury You
Beth Kevles
Temple Sinai, Washington, DC

Understanding the *Mi Shebeirach*
(May 2012)
Rabbi Lynne Landsberg
Religious Action Center of Reform Judaism, Washington, DC

Journaling/Praying
Esther M. Nathanson
Temple Sinai, Pittsburgh, Pennsylvania

A Prayer for Help
Rabbi Michele Lenke
Temple Beth Shalom, Needham, Massachusetts

Discover the Gifts
"G'vurot" and other excerpts from *Gates of Prayer: The New Union Prayerbook* © 1975
by the Central Conference of American Rabbis (CCAR) are under the copyright
protection of the Central Conference of American Rabbis and reprinted by permission
of the CCAR. All rights reserved.
Nancy Dubuar
Temple Sinai, Pittsburgh, Pennsylvania

On Loss of a Partner
Alice Shalvi
Jerusalem, Israel

Glorious Day
Sherri Feuer
Temple Israel, Minneapolis, Minnesota

SHARING OUR COVENANT | Invocations and Benedictions

A *Hineni* Prayer, As We Say Welcome
Suzy Lowinger
Temple Sinai, Delray Beach, Florida

Prayer to Open a Meeting
Marla Goldberg
Temple Beth Israel, Skokie, Illinois

The Future Is Ours
Diane Kaplan
Temple Israel, Minneapolis, Minnesota

Opening Prayer
Blair Marks
Temple Kol Emeth, Marietta, Georgia

TIME WAS: An Invocation
Lois Gibson
Temple Israel, Minneapolis, Minnesota

Invocation I
(1997)
Ellen Werther
Congregation Beth Or, Maple Glen, Pennsylvania

Invocation II
(May 2002)
Ellen Werther
Congregation Beth Or, Maple Glen, Pennsylvania

Invocation III
(May 2012)
Ellen Werther
Congregation Beth Or, Maple Glen, Pennsylvania

Invocation IV
(May 2008)
Ellen Werther
Congregation Beth Or, Maple Glen, Pennsylvania

Community Invocation for Ecumenical Dinner
"Prayer for the World" © 2003 by Rabbi Harold S. Kushner is reprinted
by permission of the author.
Jody Pascal
Congregation Beth Or, Maple Glen, Pennsylvania

Closing Prayer
Blair Marks
Temple Kol Emeth, Marietta, Georgia

SHARING OUR COVENANT | Prayers

Touch Me, God
Linda P. Zoll
Congregation Emanu El, Houston, Texas

Open Up My Heart
Originally published in *Yoga Shalom* by Lisa Levine with Carol Krucoff. New York:
URJ Press, 2011. Reprinted by permission of the URJ Press.
Cantor Lisa Levine
Temple Shalom, Chevy Chase, Maryland

Praise God
© 2000 by Barbara D. Holender
Barbara D. Holender
Temple Beth Zion, Buffalo, New York

Thank You God
Rabbi Michele Lenke
Temple Beth Shalom, Needham, Massachusetts

Avodah—In the Quiet Time of Worship
Denise Sherer Jacobson
Temple Sinai, Oakland, CA